Published 2023, in Great Britain
Copyright 2023 Women's Business Network

British Cataloguing Publication data: A catalogue record of this book is available from the British Library

Women's Business Network

Guide to Becoming a

Successful Entrepreneur

A collaboration of business advice, stories, and case studies

by the members of the

Women's Business Network for Female Entrepreneurs

sharon@womensbusinessnetworking.co.uk

CONTENTS

APPENDIX A: CONTRIBUTING AUTHORS 150

Foreword

By Kat Byles

When I first showed up to facilitate a workshop at the Women's Business Network, I was pleasantly struck by the authenticity, generosity and encouragement expressed by all of the women present. No pushy egos thrusting business cards in your face before rudely rushing off to prey on the next person. There was a warm welcome, an essence of openness. There was practical support backed by a genuine care and a desire for each woman to succeed. This is exactly what you receive in this book.

Women from the Women's Business Network sharing generously their business experience, learnings, wisdom and stories with you for the sole purpose of supporting you to thrive in your business. This collaborative, hand-up approach is a refreshing change from competitive, traditional business. It is lead by the natural warmth of founder, Sharon Louca, with her purpose to support women to succeed in business. She brings decades of management and administration experience; working the practical magic behind the scenes to ensure an enterprise runs smoothly and optimally. She has long implemented the necessary practical steps to get businesses off the ground and to grow businesses to six- and seven-figure revenues.

My experience has been that for women to thrive they need both the practical and emotional support that this book and the Women's Business Network offers. Take the UK as an example of the Western world. In 2022 under 17% of all active companies were led by women. They attracted less than 12% of the investment made in UK firms. Women-led businesses generate a lower turnover than those run by male counterparts, with average revenues of £1.3m a year, compared with £3.1m for businesses headed up by men. (Source: The Guardian reporting on The Gender Index, March 2022) For this to change, and it must, women need to lift each other up. We need to support our peers and the next generation of women to thrive in business.

Traditionally business has been a male-designed and male-lead space. When you look at the history of women entrepreneurship it is only two-to-three generations back in the fifties and sixties that the women setting up their own enterprises were pioneers. Today women are still juggling additional responsibilities, such as running a home, looking after children, or managing the declining health of elderly parents, alongside the day to day running of their business. What inspires me the most personally is that women are now changing the way that business is done. We are leading businesses with more compassion, heart, love and care for people and the planet, and this is becoming the norm. We are still pioneers.

If you are here at the beginning of your venture, or here out of the desire for more support from a community of like-minded women where you can be yourself, learn and grow, this book is a great place to start. You are alongside women who want you to succeed, who are cheering you on, and who will do all they can to help make that a reality.

Whether you are looking for wisdom on business and financial planning or journaling for inspiration. Whether it is SEO optimisation or social media marketing; making technology choices; thinking through whether to work from home or an office; or healing your relationship with money; you can read the experiences from women who have been there, done that. They are passing on their learnings so you can be in business with a little more strength and a little more confidence than you had before.

If you'd love to be part of that, read on.

To you and your business thriving.

Kat Byles.

Author, '*Creative Happy Work*': '*Follow your Heart to a Thriving Business Life and World*'. *www.KatByles.com*

Part 1

Getting Started in Business

1: Your Business Idea

By Alison Taylor

Whether you are yet to start a business or have already taken your first steps on the entrepreneurial ladder, exploring your options can open up ideas, opportunities and directions you have not yet considered.

If you are still in the dreaming stage, irritated with your current employment status, or considering a totally new direction, then read on. This chapter is your appetiser - a way of opening doors to your imagination with an array of thoughts and considerations that could ease your path into being your own boss. I wish I had read this book before I started in business. Not that I would have changed my choice of direction but I believe I would have taken myself and my business more seriously. I would have started stronger, been less hesitant and less apologetic.

What type of business do you want?

There are an infinite number of possibilities open to women in business these days. Let's begin with a series of questions. See it as a conversation with your inner self, or an overview of some of the options. I must be honest here and confess that I love what I do. I was very fortunate to happen upon a business and business model that has worked from the day I started in 2006. That does not mean the path has been an upward trajectory. Like all business owners, there have been times when I have wondered about my sanity. Serendipity did play its part. My business was initially a way to provide a financial filler for the family budget. Since that gentle start, it has gone on to provide the financial stability I sought and much more. I am still in my happy place. It must, however, be acknowledged, that 20% of start-ups will fail in the first year. That may sound like a positive statistic - 80% are succeeding but by the end of year 3, the figure of failures has risen to 60%. With only 25% ever getting to the dizzy heights of business stability after ten years. (Source: Business start-ups stats UK 2022)

It is important that you think about your business choices, including all the practical and emotional aspects of starting up and the wider implications of your decision-making. This book is aimed at helping you be one of the successful ones. Although these statistics may sound alarming, there can be a myriad of reasons as to why your business may change direction, integrate into a bigger concept, or cease trading.

Other chapters will address the importance of a sound financial strategy and strong business plan at the outset. Some of the reasons for failure in those first few years can be a poor understanding of start-up, ongoing and inflation costs, changes in government regulations, or marketplace trends overtaking ideas, to name just a few difficulties ahead. Looking at the strengths and pitfalls of each idea with crystal-clear thinking could help save you time, money and heartache.

Oliver Burkeman's book *'Four Thousand Weeks'* talks about how you approach life. He questions how you use 'the ridiculous brief time on the planet'. We do not control the future and can be liberated from anxiety by acting wisely to lessen the likelihood of bad things happening. Take heart then, your future business may not be where you expected, hoped and dreamed of in those heady start-up days but you can have a thoroughly enjoyable experience. You will be stretched intellectually, enjoy new opportunities, meet new people, become more creative and perhaps even turn a profit in those early years. Perhaps you will be one of the lucky ones. Your forward planning will help improve your odds of success and assist your good fortune.

Let us dive in and consider what your options are. Here are a few initial questions that need considering.

1. Is this a new career/direction?
2. Have you been made redundant?
3. Have you a creative itch that needs scratching?
4. Have you decided you just do not want to work for others anymore? You want to be your own boss.
5. Have you recently experienced a family/health trauma and realise life needs to change?
6. Are your outgoings exceeding your income and something needs to change?

Whatever the starting point of your research I recommend you read *Simon Sinek's* seminal work *'Start with the Why'*. Your ideas of moving away from your current pain or your desire to make the world a better place does not only rest on the practicalities of your ideas. You WILL need to dig deep and explore your values. What is important to you? Deep down, what do you stand for? For me, it was health, specifically the choices we make around a healthy lifestyle. Educating and providing the wherewithal to arrive at a way of living that allows people to flourish. My core belief is that good health is not only affordable but the foundation stone of a fulfilled life. Hence my business in in the health arena.

What have these probing questions got to do with pounds, shillings and pence you may ask? The reason is basic. Without knowing your values, your foundations will be on shaky ground. You will be tested time and time again. The world and business community around you could be supportive. It will often feel decidedly negative towards you and your work. Being clear on your values and beliefs will help you weather the inevitable storms. Goals and strategies will change. Your values will allow you to be rooted, confident in what you are aiming to achieve. It is how your customers will recognise you and the value you bring to them. Once you have thought long and hard about what you believe in, you can start to look with greater certainty about what is on offer. You will not be wasting time on business opportunities that do not align with your raison d'etre.

More questions. More decisions.

Will you be staying in employment and dipping your toe into entrepreneurship part time? Or are you going to jump in the deep end - all in! Whichever approach you take, knowing you have done your thinking and preparation first should help you find your feet. It is also worth remembering there are people in your community willing to support you and your venture. If your idea sheets are a little empty but you know you want to do something, one way to get your thoughts going is to use the Japanese concept of IKIGAI. I was introduced to this by business/life coach Ruth Dunn. Thank you, Ruth.

Ikigai has existed in Japanese culture for many years and was popularised by Japanese psychiatrist and academic *Mieko Kamiya* in her 1966 book *'On the Meaning of Life'*. Numerous examples of the Ikigai diagram can be found on the internet and there are multiple books which explain the concept in more detail.

You are taken through a series of questions.

1. What do you love?
2. What does the world need?
3. What can you be paid for?
4. What are you good at?

As you will see from the diagram below, the how and where answers to these questions can lead you to the sweet spot. It helps you discover your passions, your mission, your vocation, and your profession. Getting these ideas in balance can help you arrive at the choice that meets your needs, values and interests. Take your time over these questions. They are profound.

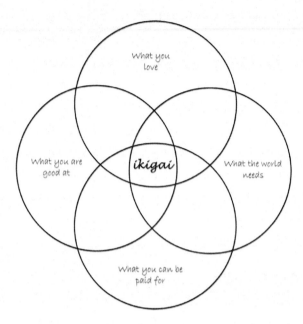

Another way to help you decide what type of business you should start is to ask your nearest and dearest. A good friend who knows you really well could prove a great sounding board.

Listen to their answers carefully. They may have hidden agendas. They may want you to keep the current status quo. Change is disruptive. You will, however, need their support. You do not have to take their advice. Asking can be a salutatory and fascinating exercise. Will they point out your flaws and shortcomings? Will they be your champion? Will they be fully behind you or worried for your security/success? Will they sit on the fence, waiting to see what transpires? Seriously, if several friends and loved ones point out a similar argument, then there may be some further exploring to be done.

Start-ups bring a new dynamic to relationships. You need to have faith in your own ability and direction and be able to share that with those close to you. They may or may not agree with your choices. It will be useful to know the thoughts of the ones close to you. Rejection is one of the realities of life; owning your own business does not protect you from this. You may even find you receive more. Such criticism can be debilitating if you allow it to be. It is not unusual to be identified with your profession or business. You may remember '*Mr Bun the Baker*'. The rejection and criticism when you are your business can suddenly feel personal.

Having a network of support can ameliorate these negative judgements. Handling rejection is the first lesson in entrepreneurship. Remember, criticism is more often not personal but a reflection of the agenda of others. Consider Mr Tesco. It is unlikely that he would go home crying if you chose to shop at Aldi. BUT he will be thinking of what he can do to keep your custom.

Let's now look at your field of interest.

- Are you pursuing an idea that is current?

- Are you passionate about your idea?

- What is the required initial investment?

- What training and skills will be needed?

- Will you want a business that is going to sustain you in the long term? Is it a business that will allow you to grow financially, intellectually, emotionally?

Here are some possible business models/ideas you could be considering.

A family business.

Joining them and/or taking the business to a new level. One business owner I met joined the sheep wool business. Not using the fleece for yarn but seeing the potential of it as an environmentally-friendly packaging material for the growing online shopping phenomena. Advantages – there will be an established trading pattern. You will have existing clients. There is a recognised brand and a wealth of experience.

The downside? Family politics!

Start from scratch.

A stand-alone business that you start at the kitchen table.

You will need to consider if this is a product or service business. The former will need more space than the kitchen table and the ingredients might have sell-by dates. Think cake businesses, cosmetics, crafts, and candles. A coaching or service-type business run from home may only require a laptop.

Advantages are lower start-up costs if premises are not initially required, and you could have the family to help. My children used to assist with labelling and delivery!

Downside - you do need to consider the impact on the family. Vying for space and having to clear away at the end of each day can cause added strain.

Product-based businesses will also need to consider regulations, sourcing and perhaps importing materials, manufacturing in larger quantities, packaging, and distribution.

Franchise

This model is extremely popular as most of the above problems are sorted for you. The downside is the initial outlay which can run into five-figure sums for very well-known and popular brands. You also do need to do your homework and use a degree of common sense.

- Do not be fooled by potential earnings.

- Ask to talk extensively with existing franchisee holders and do compare the offering of several different franchise providers.

- Be aware of annual fees, restricted areas of operation, limiting contracts, monthly payments, and final exit clauses.

Turn a hobby into a business.

You may have made things and given them away as gifts for years now and you wonder if they can be scaled up to make a going concern. Friends and family have always complimented you on your work and told you, "You should go into business."

Check!!

- Are they business owners who understand the implications of being a business owner?

- Will your hobby scale up? What quantities can you realistically make before machines or more staff need to be brought in?

- Will the hobby pay? What will your hourly rate pay? Crafts in particular can be very time-consuming to make. Will the public pay a realistic price for your time as well as materials and overheads?

- Where will you sell? Stall costs vary. So too does their popularity and success. Online sales are time-consuming and may require additional staffing to work efficiently.

- Could you turn your hobby or craft into a workshop/demonstrations/teaching idea? Thereby reaching a wider audience and working more effectively.

Network Marketing.

These companies abound and one business colleague states with confidence, "Everyone should have a network marketing business." I must declare an interest, as this is where I started. It has worked for me since 2006. As with all the other choices discussed here, you must choose a product or service that fires your interest. Again, do your homework. Talk to people who have had success and those who have not. Seek out for yourself what you think makes a business work for some and not others. Ask those pertinent questions. Of course. This is lifelong learning in action! Much better to be thorough at this stage than to spend time, money and emotion on something that was not fully thought through. You only have to watch *'The Apprentice'* interviews to see how fragile some ideas are.

Ask yourself what is popular now. What are the trends? What are people searching for? Check out all the social media platforms and see what is gaining traction. 'Ask.com' is another very useful tool for spotting trends. Do you want to follow a trend putting your own spin on it? For example, there is always a market for cakes. Remember to consider the start-up costs, ingredients, fuel, and the competition locally. How will you find your niche? What about the trends toward healthy food choices and/or veganism? Has this peaked or do you have a novel take on what can be offered?

Gin? How many more flavours can there be? What about the other spirits or the low alcohol market?

Coaching? This is a huge arena. If in your previous life you have led a team, been responsible for managing projects, or been involved in training, you will undoubtedly have developed a raft of skills. Again, please do your research. Who would you want to coach, why, and how?

Environmental/social concerns. The world is crying out for solutions to any number of problems. Transport, water shortage, climate change. The list is endless. Do you have a solution that could be monetised?

Future-gazing. Not so much as to what is popular now but more of a 'what the world needs now is...'. What do people, families, women, children, fathers, and the elderly need? Do you have the seed of an idea that could make the lives of any group easier? Originality is understandably rare but if you can dream, fulfil a yawning gap in the market, and bring your idea to fruition, the world will beat a path to your door.

We go back to what are you passionate about? What are your skills? What values will underpin your idea? What gems can you share and bring to the marketplace? Above all, who do you want to help? Are you in this for the long haul? Have you got the stamina?

The joy of a happy customer, the ringing of the till, and the glow of a great testimonial are not to be underestimated.

Do let us know what you decide.

2: The Importance of Having a Business Plan

By Wendy Garcarz

My first business was an independent florist shop, I knew I needed premises, a delivery van, and staff to get **'Wendy's of Weston'** up and running. I was a first-class florist, with five years' experience in a very busy high street retail store, and I had a bit of capital, just enough to get me off the ground, but no spare money if there was a problem.

I put together my first business plan because my bank manager said he wouldn't open a business account for me until he saw one. So, I used the template in the business start-up pack he gave me at the end of our interview and just filled in the boxes. On paper, it looked fine, my business account was set up and I started trading within the week, well it was 1985! Unsurprisingly, I experienced the six most common, small-business problems before my first business folded. If I had completed the business plan properly, I could have avoided that painful lesson.

The six most common small business problems

1. I had a full order book, but terrible cashflow. All of my suppliers were paid as I bought my stock, but invoices for funeral flowers, restaurants I supplied and large functions had typically 14-28 days to pay. I was offering the same payment terms as the national chain I had worked for previously, even though I was a small business, working on much smaller profit margins.

2. I couldn't be in two places at once, so I needed delivery drivers to deliver what I was making, and because my competitors gave free delivery, I didn't have a delivery charge either. I didn't know what I should be charging as I didn't know how to accurately calculate that. I charged roughly the same or slightly less than my competitors in order to win business. I didn't understand why I was barely breaking even yet working so hard.

3. I knew my business was seasonal; Valentine's Day, Mother's Day and Christmas were great, but how did I pay my bills in the quieter periods? I had no idea. I didn't have a budget!

4. My wastage was high. I was worried about not having exactly what people wanted when they walked through the door, but I kept poor records and could only say anecdotally what my best sellers were. That meant I bought stock on instinct rather than by identifying sales trends.

5. I had a beautifully sign-written van and a sign over the shop door, and believed my customers would all come from passing by. I had no sales or marketing plan or budget for those activities.

6. My business was run on gut reaction and my skills as a florist, there was no analysis or understanding of my market, no knowledge about how the entity that is a business runs, what it needs, or how to make a success of it. I was armed with a little knowledge, good skills, and bags of enthusiasm. I set my business up and HOPED I was doing enough of the right things to make it work. I wasn't.

I believed that as long as I worked really hard it would all be ok, but it doesn't matter how many hours you put in if you are doing the wrong things. When my business inevitably closed, I went back to the bank manager to close my account and he gave me the single most valuable piece of business advice I have ever had, *"Hope is not a business strategy."* He was right, I had not been in control of any aspect of that business and as a result I was powerless to do anything but fail.

Why you need a business plan

A business plan gives the power back to you because it puts you in charge of what happens to your business and helps you to combat those things that affect your business. A good plan makes you ask the right questions (the ones that your market will expect you to know the answers to). It will give you a structure and help you focus your activities in the areas that make money, not lose it.

If you want your business to have a strong foundation; financially and operationally

Most high street or online banks will want to see a written business plan before they take you on. A description of your business idea is not enough. They want to see you have put some thought into your idea, researched your target market and understand what the cost of running your business will be.

If you want to make sound decisions that manage risks in your business

A business plan is a practical document that helps you understand what you need to do to make your business flourish. It identifies the decisions and actions that help and identifies those that masquerade as important but create waste or slow down progress. It should cover the four important areas of a business: finance, operations, sales, and people.

If you want to spot the bear traps and any weaknesses in your business

A business plan will pose a series of questions that check you have thought of the eventualities that may affect your business. Planning takes the guesswork out of running a business. By thinking about the things that might happen; problems with your supply chain, raw materials shortage, fuel price increases etc, you can have a contingency to counteract the effects on your business.

If you want to create a steady income with a steady stream of new clients

A business plan is a sales tool that helps you to clearly identify who your target market (ideal customer) is and where they hang out. This will help you to aim your marketing messages directly at them improving the connection you have and increasing your conversion rate from prospect to actual trading customers.

How to do it

Creating a business plan involves research and some thought, all of which, is time well spent. You need to consider why you do what you do and use that as a starting point. It does not need to be complicated. At its core, your plan should identify where you are now, where you want your business to go and how you will get there. Writing a good business plan does not guarantee success, but it can go a long way toward reducing the odds of failure. It helps to write your plan through a series of questions that you write detailed answers to. The way your plan is presented is of secondary importance to the quality of thinking and analysis that goes into it.

1. **Identify and put into words your 'why'.**

   Why are you in business and what difference do you make to your customers? This takes some thought because it's asking you to define the thing that drives you in your business. **HINT**: the answer is not money - that is an output of business, a reward if you like. This is the sort of stuff that when people say it about you, it gives you goosebumps. Your why is your very purpose, the thing that keeps you doing what you do in the face of adversity. My why is inspiring people to break through limiting beliefs and to do things they never thought possible. Now, there's a sentence you don't see in many business plans! Use this section to articulate the value that you bring to your customers' lives that they don't get elsewhere and that they identify specifically with you.

2. **Describe your business.**

What do you do and how do you do it?

HINT: This is the content that appears on your website and marketing/social media posts that describes your product or service, your values, the things you consider important in the way that you do business with your customers.

You can also include your product/service features and benefits here too.

3. **Perform a basic market analysis.**

Who are your main competitors and how do you differ from what they offer the market?

HINT: Stand back and examine your market as a whole. What is it worth?

- How is it broken down (market segments)?
- Market trends; is it growing, static, or in decline?
- Is there healthy competition or is it saturated with providers?

Then, focus on your niche of the market and ask the same questions. Identify the market demographics, what is the profile of your customers in terms of income, age, gender, lifestyle, aspirations etc. Armed with Google you can do one of these in 1-2 hours and it really is time well spent.

1. **Write down how your business runs**

By writing this obvious stuff down it helps you to see your business as your customers would.

HINT: How do people find you? In premises, online, recommendation, advertising etc. How do you deliver your goods/services? Consider the values as well as the practical operations you need to deliver to your customers. What are the important processes in your business that affect quality and customer service? Do you have terms and conditions that set out your payment terms, contractual requirements, cancellations, complaints, and service guarantees clearly? These can prevent costly problems and disputes later on.

2. **The pricing model for your products and services**

What are your offerings (packages) and how do you group them to meet your customers' needs?

HINT: this section helps you to understand your market position.

Example: are you a 'Lidl' moving high volumes at low prices?

Are you a 'Tesco' offering a wide range at a reasonable cost to cover as many customers as possible? Are you a 'Waitrose' offering a luxury brand, moving smaller quantities of high value product, with added service value? Lack of clarity here can seriously damage profitability. You will not make money selling Waitrose level service at Tesco Prices.

3. **Perform some customer segmentation**

   Understand what makes your customers tick. CLUE: how many types of clients do you have and who buys what from you? What are their main problems, and how do you solve them?

4. **Write a basic marketing plan**

   Describe your intended marketing/advertising activities for the coming year.

   HINT: describe how you will reach, attract and persuade customers to buy your products or services, identify the channels you will use (online, face to face, networking), and where your customers hang out (which social media platforms they use). Design content that helps them choose you. Do you know how often a prospect comes into contact with your business before they become a paying customer? Is your branding clear and easily identifiable with you?

5. **Create a budget and financial plan**

   Identify what it costs to run your business, all your costs and overheads, and then create an operating budget to help you manage your cashflow.

   HINT: write down all the costs related to running your business (salaries/drawings, premises, vehicles, energy, communications, computers, raw materials, insurances, licenses, professional fees, HR, tax, NI, book-keeping, admin support, EVERYTHING! Then devise a simple budget that splits that into 12 monthly payments. Look at how much profit you need to make to pay all of that and create a surplus for emergencies. Understanding that will ensure you know how much you need to make every month to keep a healthy financial balance.

6. **Monitor your performance by being accountable**

   Monitoring your performance is key to success. It helps you to spot problems early and deal with them before they become a crisis. It can also help you to make better decisions, reduce waste, and develop new income streams by responding to the trends in your market.

   HINT: know your break-even point and your profit margins, set realistic targets, and check on them regularly, (at least monthly). Check compliments and complaints (service quality) and have an accountability buddy that helps you to review your business objectively (good accountant, a business buddy or coach). Accountability works when there is trust, honesty, and respect. You need to trust that the person will treat your information with confidentiality and discretion. You need to be honest with that person so that there is no judgement, just objectivity and a desire to see you succeed. You need to respect the person so that you take anything they say seriously, and you learn from them.

Devising your business plan is not a waste of time, but a genuine investment in your future. It doesn't matter what it looks like, whether you use a template or produce a beautiful glossy leaflet. The value of a good business plan is the research and thinking that goes into it. Keep it simple and ask yourself the basic/obvious questions as a starting point. Talk to other business people and get their take on your market, product, or service. It is easier to grow a profitable business when you minimise the amount of unpredictable stuff you deal with. A business plan takes the guesswork out of running a business. Since that first disaster, every business I have run has had a plan, some more sophisticated than others *(depending on the business)*. Those businesses have succeeded despite recessions, inflation, and pandemics.

"An hour of planning can save you ten hours of doing"

Dale Carnegie

3: Business Planning - Build a Financial Plan for your Future

By Karen Hagan

Setting up financial goals

One of the first things you should do when starting out in business is write down your financial goals. What do you want to achieve financially out of your business?

Get a large piece of paper and brain-dump all your dreams, goals, and visions, for you, your loved ones, and your family. Imagine yourself in 5 years' time, where do you want to be? Perhaps in your dream home? Perhaps having two really good holidays a year? Travelling to places you have always wanted to go to? Having the financial freedom to work part-time or a 4-day week? What about securing your children's future? Maybe giving them deposits for their first home? Make these goals personal to you and get them down on paper. Now start to divide them up into 1-year, 3-year and 5-year goals. Maybe even go as far as 10 years if you feel like it!

Retirement goals

Think about when you want to retire. Will you be stopping work entirely one day, or will it be a gradual slow-down, e.g., reducing how many days you work each week? Write it down and then you can factor this into your business plan.

£s and sales

Now work out what your average sale is in pounds. Firstly, look at your total income from sales in one month, then take the number of products (or services) you have sold in one month and divide the income by the number of sales. This gives you a figure which is your average sale in pounds.

Survival budget

Your next step is to work out what you need to earn from your business. Let's work it out using a 'survival budget'. Start with creating an outgoings sheet – this should list all your necessary household and personal expenses in a whole month. Make sure these are just the essentials e.g., the mortgage/rent, utilities, council tax, food, just the basics. Don't include lifestyle expenses like holidays or leisure, cinema, going out, etc. Total up this figure and make a note of it.

Now do a household income sheet but ignore any income you currently bring into the household from your business. Include income from your partner or your second job. What is the deficit between the outgoings sheet total and this income total? As an example, if your outgoings are £2,000 per month and your household income is £1,500 per month, then there is a deficit of £500 per month. Your deficit is the amount you need to earn from your business as a minimum. Anything extra is a bonus.

The benefit of doing this 'survival budget' is that it takes the pressure off you to earn anything extra. If you can comfortably earn the minimum needed to keep a roof over your head and pay the bills, then this means you can open your mind to growing your business and working 'on' it and not just 'in' it - working your butt off just to pay the bills each month.

Keep a note of this 'deficit' figure and aim to at least always earn this as a minimum each month. How many sales is this, based on the average sale value? How many sales per week do you need to make? If you are struggling to meet this figure, then consider increasing your prices or consider upselling further packages to your already-existing clients.

Tracking money

Let's return to that average sale amount. I'd advise you to keep a spreadsheet to track the average sale over a 12-month period. Ideally you need to see the average sale amount per customer increasing over time. This means you are doing less work for more income as time goes on.

Your plan

You now have the basics of a business financial plan. You can return to this regularly to see:

- Are my finances static, up or down?
- Track your money: Where is it coming from? Where is it going? What do I really need to earn?
- Where can I cut to save money without affecting customer experience and generate a development fund?

A development fund is important, to have the means to invest in yourself and to 'sharpen the saw'. This means staying up to date with trends in your market and keeping your skills current and continuously developing yourself. This is vital to keep your business growing and not to get stagnant.

Tracking your business figures

Use Cashflow Forecast sheets and Sales Projections sheets – these can be Googled and found on the internet for free. Complete them regularly and this way you can 'track your money' within your business. Keep tabs on where it's going. Work out your income into the business and your regular outgoings from it. There are chapters dedicated to money, accounting and finance in this book.

On the subject of keeping records, make sure you record all expenses you incur as part of the business. If you work from home this can even include some of your utility bills. Don't forget that even personal development costs can be included as an expense of the business, for example if you buy self-help books these can be a business expense if they are related to the growth of your business.

Ensure your business cashflow is smooth and that this doesn't cause you any problems. Most businesses that fail do so because of poor cashflow. The easiest way to resolve this is to shorten your payment terms i.e., make invoices payable within 14 days. Keep a record of leads and conversions. Note where your leads are coming from. Do they convert to business? How often? If not then why not? Are your leads coming from one particular networking group but not from others? Consider the return on your investment – are these groups worth the cost?

Accounting

Make sure you use a really good accountant. This is vital and you should do your homework and get one who is proactive and who you get on well with. Your accountant shouldn't be someone you only speak to once a year when it's tax return filing time. They should communicate with you regularly and alert you to tax-saving opportunities and check in with you on a frequent basis.

Saving

Save 30% of your income on 'pay-day'. You need to do this to ensure that you meet tax deadlines and have the money easily available to pay any tax bill. By saving 30% of your income, you will not only easily cover your tax and National Insurance bill but you should also have a small emergency fund building up for your business. This is really important, and especially if your work is seasonal you should think about saving more when work is plentiful, for those times when work dries up.

Future-proof your business

Keep reviewing your Business Plan – set a date in your diary every 3 months as if it is client work. This date is non-negotiable and must happen!

Reconsider your pricing. Consider if there is scope to increase your prices.

Know your worth!

Delegate and outsource where necessary – you cannot do everything yourself! Your time is better spent growing your business and servicing your clients because that is what YOU are best at.

Track your spreadsheets

You will learn valuable business information from doing this.

- Review surveys and feedback from clients every three months.
- Regularly update your website.
- Keep a journal – journaling is useful to track your wins, challenges, focus and learnings.

I have written a chapter dedicated to journaling in part two of this book.

Use these headings too for a yearly overview sheet and complete this at the end of each year.

Marketing budget

Develop a Marketing Budget and keep a spreadsheet of how, when and where you will market and what this will cost. Is this a valuable use of your budget and what is the return on investment?

Think about direct mail as a marketing strategy. This can reap huge rewards and can be a great return on your investment. TIP: If you are a professional services provider, consider taking on 'pro bono' clients, e.g., for free. Treat it as paid marketing and insist on a testimonial when the transaction is completed.

Futureproof your finances

Protect your income. Your business can pay for Executive Income Protection. This pays you a salary if you are sick and unable to work long-term. If you were suffering from a long-term illness, think about who could step in and run your business. Discuss with people as to what would happen in this situation and put some plans in place. You wouldn't want to leave your customers with no-one to continue that relationship with them, would you?

What if you were diagnosed with a critical illness? Many business owners return to work too soon because they need to earn a living but it's also important to have time to rest and recover properly. Critical Illness insurance can make the difference as it gives you breathing space with a tax-free lump sum to see you through a period of recovery.

Have you gone into business with a business partner?

Consider taking out Shareholder Protection – this protects your family if you die and ensures your share of the value of the business you have created passes to who you want it to. Your business partner's spouse or your spouse may not want any involvement in the business but if you don't put protection in place, they will inherit your share of it. My message to all business owners is that sometimes the worst can happen. None of us want to think about that but it can and does happen from time to time, and you need to take steps to protect you, your family, and the business you have worked hard to create, so get some help with this from a financial adviser.

Your business is growing – what next?

Now you have a growing business are you employing people?

Think about employment law and get independent HR advice.

Also consider outsourcing payroll as this can be complicated and time-consuming.

Ensure you are using an up-to-date accountancy package to comply with tax or other legislation. If you employ staff, you will need to provide a registered pension scheme and pay into this for them under Auto Enrolment requirements by law. Consider taking out Private Medical Insurance so that if you need medical care or treatment this can be quickly sorted out – it can also be paid for by the business. Now that your income is increasing you should be paying into a personal pension, as either regular monthly payments or as a lump sum at the end of your financial year. Get financial advice on this too as it's so important. Women tend to put others first and don't always prioritise looking after their own wealth. You must protect and maximise the money you have worked hard to create!

4: Understanding Your Relationship with Money

By Kim Masters

If I ask you to write a list of five things that you constantly worry about, I guess that money will feature. It may even be top of your list.

When you look at money in its simplest form, it's just numbers, bits of metal and paper, a tool for exchange of goods and services. But it's become much bigger than that, it's this monster that has taken over our lives. As a society, money is the focus; it starts when we are young and are deciding what we want to be when we grow up. We give up the dreams to become more practically-minded, and what's the reason for that? Money.

I wanted to be a journalist when I was growing up, but my mum and dad went to great lengths to show me how hard it would be to make money, and how I would struggle. My dad even went as far as to buy me a book on budgeting. I ended up studying bookkeeping and accounting, which as it's turned out is not too bad, because I've managed to turn it into a passion, which is to help people. Once we are on our career path, the next step is the quest to earn money, to get as much as we can so we can live comfortably and buy all the things we need. This quest becomes all-encompassing and impacts our decision-making. What decisions have you made where money was the overriding, or only consideration? What was your motivation for starting your own business? Yes, we all want to make money, me included, but so many people I talk to start a business with money as the main motivating factor. They only want to work with wealthy people so they can charge more and make more money. I understand this logic, however it has its pitfalls. People with money are usually very particular who they give it to, and their expectations are extremely high, so they're not a pushover.

For me, any business must start with passion and a will to make a difference in people's lives. I believe that money will then come naturally. The primary driving force for me is in helping people first and making money second. When money is the focus you risk missing other opportunities, and your clients can sense that it's not really about them.

I want you to stop and ask yourself this question, "How much money do I really need to live comfortably?" We don't need millions to survive, we just think we do. We live in a society that constantly sells us an ideal lifestyle, we are constantly bombarded with adverts telling us what we need to buy, what we can't live without, tempting bargains, and the huge amounts of 'life-changing' money we can win. We all get sucked into this vortex created by the money monster, it's hungry, and it's coming for you, it will take all you have, and leave you slogging away for more.

The key area I work with people on is their relationship with money. This is how you think, feel, speak, and act around money. Think about your relationship with money, do you always complain about how expensive things are? Do you worry about not having enough money? Do you dream about what you'll spend your lottery winnings on? Do you feel bitter and jealous when you see people with more money than you? Do you spend money faster than you can make it? Don't worry, lots of people have this sort of relationship with money. What I want to highlight right now is that having a negative relationship with money can have an impact on your mental health, physical health, your relationships with others, your actions, and your behaviour. You end up with tunnel vision, with head down as you plough ahead.

By healing your relationship with money, you open yourself up to so many possibilities, new relationships, you feel better in your mind and your body, but most importantly it opens you up to a whole new level of creativity and abundance, it removes the blinkers, raises your head so you can see all the potential opportunities around you, it makes you more confident, and gives you control of your own life. This is so important when you are running your own business. Once you start exploring your own relationship with money, you'll be amazed at what you will uncover. It's like clearing out a wardrobe and finding items of clothing you forgot you had, and don't remember buying. You may even ask yourself, "What was I thinking!?"

It's like that with money, when you start rooting around in your subconscious, you start finding lots of emotional money baggage that you forgot was there, or don't even remember having. Some of this baggage can seem so absurd you wonder what you were thinking, and how it got there.

At this point it's important to understand the roles of the conscious and subconscious minds. Imagine an iceberg, the conscious mind is the bit at the top that's exposed, where logic, short-term memory, willpower, and critical thinking live. The next stage is called the preconscious, which is just below the waterline, where the information that we call upon occasionally is stored. The best example is when someone asks you for your telephone number.

You can remember it, but it's not something you think about all the time. The subconscious is the huge mass of ice below the surface, the bit we don't see. It's where our imagination, beliefs, creativity, emotions, feelings, intuition, long-term memory, values, and protective reactions live.

The subconscious is like a filing cabinet which is full of life memories and experiences. There is so much stored there that we can't possibly be aware of it all. Sometimes we don't even know something is stored there. Your parents may have talked about how expensive everything was, or how hard they had to work to get money. Now, you won't necessarily have made a conscious decision to store these memories, because a lot of the time the brain just does it for you. Then whenever money is discussed, the brain goes to your filing cabinet, pulls out the money file, and reads all the notes on how expensive things are, and how hard you must work for money, which then affects how you think and act around money. Someone else's beliefs have now become yours.

When you understand this, you soon learn that in order to get a grip on money, you have to dive below the surface and explore the filing cabinet that is the subconscious. You never know what you will find, but there can be some gremlins hiding down there that could be having a huge, negative impact on your life. It's even more important to do this when you are running your own business because you need to be in a state of open-mindedness and creativity, as this encourages growth. If you have negative money beliefs, they can really hold you back; it could even lead your business to fail.

Some people struggle to earn over a certain level. No matter what they try, they just can't get past it. This is a common negative belief called an 'earnings ceiling'. It's where your subconscious has set a limit to how much you think you can earn. You can try marketing plans, social media campaigns, and cost-controlling, but until that limiting belief is dealt with, you'll struggle to progress.

A previous client was a young lady who was running a catering business. When we met, she was trying to get investment, but not getting anywhere. The lightbulb moment was when she told me, "Money isn't real." It's an odd statement, but it made a lot of sense. Whenever she was running out of money, she would ask her mum for more, and mum obliged by giving her money. Money had no meaning for my client, it was just something her mum kept giving her. There were no real consequences because mum just kept writing the cheques, and she wasn't worried about cost management or job costing. As soon as we sat down and cleared the money block, she transformed into another person. She put all the practical financial tools in place, and within months was talking to serious investors and received the funding she needed to move to larger premises.

Another area I focus on is negative money habits. We all have them, spending on credit cards, shopping to make us feel better, buying stuff we don't need, sales shopping, ignoring the credit card statement, not checking our bank account regularly, there are loads of them.

Just like negative beliefs, bad money habits can be destructive. Another client I worked with had experienced a business deal that lost him lots of money. Because of that experience he refused to open any post from his bank, he was afraid to read the letters because the past trauma made him think all letters from the bank were bad news, and so he binned them.

It's an important exercise to try and figure out your money habits, even the small ones. As *Benjamin Franklin* once said,

> *"Beware of little expenses. A small leak will sink a great ship."*

Small bad habits can have the same effect.

Running a business is challenging, the main problem I see time and again is that people don't give the numbers enough respect and time they deserve. It's not the glamorous side of business, it's seen as boring, but trust me when I say that this is one belief you must change as a business owner.

It's vitally important that you have proper systems and procedures in place where accounting is concerned; you simply can't run a good business without it. Accurate, up-to-date accounts will tell you everything you need to know about your business. It's the script, the story, it can be a comedy, a drama, or an action film, but what you don't want is for it to become a horror. A lot of businesses fail because people didn't care enough about the numbers, it was someone else's problem. Pass a pile of paper to the accountant and let them sort it out.

Another previous client, an events company, had a finance manager. As far as the directors were concerned, the numbers were telling them they were making a profit. The problem was that the finance manager was struggling. The directors asked him if he needed help, but he said he was fine. Suddenly the finance manager left. When I was called in it took months to sort out the accounts, they were in a complete mess. When the dust settled the picture was not the romantic comedy they thought it was, it was a horror, they were making a loss of hundreds of thousands of pounds! Thankfully the directors acted quickly, and we were able to rescue the situation, but just imagine the consequences if things hadn't changed.

Summary:

- Understanding your relationship with money will have a positive impact on your personal and business life.
- Negative money beliefs and money blocks can stop growth.

- You can change your money story by replacing old, negative beliefs with new, positive ones.

- You must learn to put time and effort into your accounts.

- Take the time to learn some basic accounting terminology and skills.

- Yes, you can outsource your accounts, but it doesn't mean you can turn your back on them.

- Your finances are your responsibility, own them.

- Learn to love money. It can be a source of great joy, excitement, and growth. You don't have to fear it.

- Ask yourself, how much money do I need to be happy?

5: Multiple Streams of Income

By Vicky Farmer

Have you heard the saying *'Don't put all your eggs in one basket'*? It refers to the danger of putting all your delicate items in one place and losing the lot in a single instance if you trip and drop them all. When it comes to our working life, most of us work for someone else as an employee and build a career. That's certainly what I did. I studied hard at school, got good A-Level results and went to university. I came out with a law degree and trained as a Chartered Accountant. Surely that was my future all sewn up, working my way up the accountancy profession? I never considered anything else; that is until, after 30 years, I was made redundant. That was the moment my eggs went tumbling to the ground and smashed into a massive omelette. I didn't have another option.

I could have looked for another job in the accountancy profession, but after 30 years I didn't see why I should take on a job that I had been doing 20 years ago and for half the salary I was worth. It's at that point that I first learned the importance of having multiple income streams. It's all about spreading your risk and NOT putting all your eggs in that basket. There are many ways of going about this and my way was a bit accidental, although I did refine it later on.

Life after redundancy

Being made redundant is a bit of a life-changer especially when you think you have a good career and a job for life, but it just goes to show how precariously we are all positioned. In fact, my first thought when I was given the news was, *"Why couldn't they have waited a couple of years so our mortgage would have been paid off?"* But that wasn't the case, so I just had to get on with it and one week later I would have to go in and clear my desk.

In the meantime, I met up with a friend who told me about a business networking meeting she was going to that same morning, and she asked me if I would like to go with her. "Why not" I thought. The idea of business networking was completely new to me and I'm so glad I went.

At the meeting, about 20 women were sitting around a big table and each had 60 seconds to tell everyone about their business. When it was my turn, I stood up and told everyone how I didn't have a business, but I had been made redundant and was on my way to clear my desk. The open mouths and audible gasps around the room took me by surprise, and at that point I learned that I had a very important characteristic – resilience. I wasn't going to let this life-changing event beat me and at the age of 50, I was ready for a complete career change. But what?

For the most part, we need to work to earn money so we can cover our day-to-day expenses and, hopefully, have some left over for those treats like meals out, theatre trips and holidays. What was I going to do? This is when I discovered the world of Multi-Level Marketing or Direct Sales as it is often referred to. This is a subject that is surrounded by controversy, so all I will say at this point is – you don't know what it's like until you've tried it! Yet there are many critics who have absolutely no experience whatsoever. If you aren't familiar with this type of business model, there is a dedicated chapter on this topic (Chapter 11) that I urge you to read to help you develop an informed opinion.

For me, it was an affordable, quick, and easy way to set up my own business and start earning straight away. All marketing materials were provided at very low cost and the personal development and business training that was provided completely free was invaluable. I may have had 30 years' experience as an accountant, advising others on how to manage their businesses, but I had no practical experience of running a business or how to sell, and to attend courses to learn all this would have cost a fortune. Plus, there is no substitute for learning on the job. The flexibility was also very much appreciated as it enabled me to develop a good work-life balance.

The business I chose to join was called Pampered Chef and involved demonstrating high-end kitchen gadgets in people's homes in order to sell them. Cooking, and food in general, was a subject I was really interested in and that is so important when choosing a business. I was offered a number of different types of business opportunities by various friends and colleagues when I was looking to start out, but I knew I had to gravitate towards something I believed in and enjoyed if I was going to be successful. The thought of feeling enthusiastic about utility bills or candles was not doing it for me, but cooking and food was more my thing - and it turned out I was quite good at it. I learned that I was skilled at selling without being pushy. What's more, my customers loved the products and were happy to recommend me. I had found my perfect place – where work didn't feel like work, and I even looked forward to Monday mornings. At this point, I had also taken on a part-time post at a university, supervising students on their Masters' programme for accounting and finance, and I also had a few accountancy clients on a self-employed basis. I had found my multiple income streams, and I also had my own business, which left me feeling in control of my life.

Looking at things differently

One thing about being self-employed is that it can be seen as being a bit unpredictable in terms of job security. But actually, I look at it a different way. When you are self-employed, you are in control. You decide when you work, how you work and who you work with. You can't do any of this when you are employed by someone else, and you are totally at their mercy if they decide they don't want or need you to work for them anymore – as I had already found out after 30 years in a so called 'job for life'.

The one aspect of self-employment that probably scares people most is the uncertainty around business coming in. After all, you can have the best product or service offering in the world, but if you have no customers, it counts for nothing. But in my opinion, that's actually what makes it more secure than being employed, as long as you can crack the marketing side of things, because life in business is like a roller coaster – you need to learn to cling on for the highs and ride out the lows. That said, you need to stay focused, and you need to stick at it. It's a well-known fact that whereas almost 90% of new UK businesses survive the first 12 months, less than 40% are still there after 5 years according to data recorded. (Source: Statista October 2022)

After six years of learning how to run my own business and growing my own client base, I felt that I needed to focus on the one thing I enjoyed most, and which brought in the most money. I felt I was ready to concentrate on that and work on building it up as my main business, so I chose to put everything into Pampered Chef. And therein lies a salutary tale. Within three months of informing the university that I no longer wished to work with them and passing on most of my accountancy clients to other accountants, Pampered Chef announced it would be closing the business in the UK. All I had left to show for over six years of effort was a list of 2,000 customers. My one remaining income stream was gone.
Talk about learning the hard way!

This is always a risk with multi-level marketing businesses or franchises compared with something you have built up from the ground yourself. At the time, I was prepared to take that risk as I knew it would give me a quicker way to get to a point of earning a meaningful income, and if nothing else, it would teach me many lessons to be able to start again should the need arise. This time, I did not turn my back on the need for multiple income streams but instead used it to create my own brand.

Starting over – again!

I had always had an interest in food and nutrition and decided the time had come to retrain, with a view to becoming a health and nutrition coach. The more I learned about nutrition, the more I realised it was more than just advising people about their eating habits. Most people would benefit from a more holistic approach including supplementation, skincare, and even advice on improving their environment to reduce their exposure to the harmful chemicals hiding in plain sight in their homes.

By developing a service to provide health coaching, I also decided to add in a few product lines to complement it. I gravitated towards direct sales brands because despite my previous unfortunate experience, I did consider it an easy way to operate as a small business with low start-up costs, with due diligence already done and no need to hold stock in favour of direct shipping. I also felt that I was able to offer better quality products at affordable prices as a result of dealing directly with the manufacturers, and no distributors or wholesalers taking their cut. It also meant that as the result of creating my own brand that included an integrated product range, if any of my suppliers decided to pull out of the market, I would simply replace them seamlessly with a carefully chosen alternative. And that is how I have made multiple income streams work for me.

The reality is, without the push of redundancy, I don't think I would have jumped ship completely from employment. But if I had known back then what I know now, I would have looked into adding on at least one extra income stream, even if it was something I did very part-time and kept it ticking over like a dormant volcano, ready to burst forth at a moment's notice. That way, when the inevitable happened, and my so-called job for life was pulled out from under me, I would have been able to hit the ground running with a seamless transition from employment to self-employment, without a period of unemployment in between and all the uncertainty and stress that goes with it.

Clearly, I have learned a few lessons along the way, and I do believe that what I have ended up with works well for me. You could even think about turning a hobby into something that generates an income. After all, if you do something you really enjoy, it won't even feel like work. Don't be like me and wait until you are almost at retirement age before taking a positive step. Make the most of your time to start planning now and you never know.

6: Pricing Your Products or Services

By Wendy Garcarz

One of the most frequent issues I deal with when working with female business owners is their pricing strategy. Many of them worry they are charging too much for their products or services and are fearful of how they can justify what they charge. What is interesting is that I have rarely had to deal with this as an issue with male business owners. This suggests to me that what we are dealing with is as much a money mindset issue as it is a pricing issue.

For me, knowing my worth means three things:

1. Being confident in the rates I charge because I have used a formula to work out the price rather than copying my competitors.

2. Being clear about my business model so I know I am using a sound financial formula.

3. Being unapologetic about collecting those rates.

It is time for female entrepreneurs to stop battling the financial stereotypes that goes back decades. It's generally true that salaried women still earn less on average than men in many sectors. As business owners, especially those who provide professional services, we are in a unique position to set our own rates. We should do that from a position of confidence in ourselves and our businesses.

Perfect pricing is not an art or a science, but a combination of business awareness and self-confidence. Charge too much and you can scare off your clients but charge too little and you devalue your services. Being confident in your pricing means understanding four key factors and how they work together to set your price. monitor progress or spot problems early.

Market positioning should dictate your pricing strategy

You need to decide what position your business occupies in your market sector and that will guide your pricing.

Basically, every business sector is split into three levels.

- **The Low-cost Level**: where a business provides a no-frills service at a basic cost but handles high volumes in order to generate good revenue. Customers expect less choice, basic service and packaging, and generally see this as a disposable, short-lived purchase. Examples include Aldi (supermarket), Primark and Poundland (retail).

- **The Middle Ground:** where a business provides a broad choice to most users at an average cost. Customers expect good availability of choice, periodic special offers (they love a bargain from time to time) and a reasonable level of service that may be affected by peak trading times. Examples include Tesco/Morrisons (supermarket), Direct Line (insurance comparison site) Vauxhall/Ford/KIA (car manufacturer).

- **Luxury Level:** where a business provides a luxury product that services a small but higher-value customer base. Bespoke, tailored services that meet the customer's specification would be included in this level. Customers see this as a lifestyle choice and have very high expectations of all aspects of their transaction. They will want high-quality marketing, personalised customer service (no waiting), luxury packaging, quick and easy payment, and in return will expect to pay a higher premium for the service. Examples include Waitrose (supermarket), Rolex/Louis Vuitton (designer label), Tesla, Jaguar (car manufacturer).

Basic maths tells you that it is more costly to provide a luxury service than a budget service and although these examples are national companies, the same principles apply to independently owned businesses. Understanding how you want to position your business is vital to ensure the price that you settle on delivers your business goals. I have seen too many business owners plough huge amounts of time and resources into their customer service, packaging, and after sales care, yet their prices match the pile-it-high-sell-it-cheap companies that share their market sector. Understanding what the business costs to run is the starting point for your price. Before you set your price, you need to understand your costs of providing these services to customers.

- **Materials costs.** These are the costs of goods you use in providing the service. A cleaning business would need to factor in costs of paper towels, cleaning solutions, rubber gloves, etc. An auto repair business would include the cost of supplies and parts, such as brake fluid and pads, which are being installed by service people. Tradespeople will often include a material list of everything they will use as part of their estimate when bidding for jobs.

- **Labour costs**. This is the cost of direct labour or time involved in providing that service. This might be the hourly wages of a cleaning crew, or the time spent coaching a person or producing a report for a client. It is vital that this is an accurate cost as estimates invariably fall short and can erode any profit from a job.

- **Overhead costs.** These are the indirect costs that your business incurs daily. Examples include administrative costs, monthly rent, taxes, insurance, depreciation, advertising, office supplies, utilities, mileage, etc. During turbulent times (recession, inflation increases) you should not depend on historical figures to calculate this but calculate them using current figures to ensure you protect profit margins in the business.

- **Profit margins**. Profit is one of the main indicators of business performance. With lots of money flowing in and out of your business, it's not always clear how much money you're making. By calculating profit over a set period, you can keep an eye on the health of your business.

Once you determine your costs, you need to mark up your services to ensure that you achieve a profit for your business. The profit is the money earned by the business and is used to create a surplus (in leaner times), fund any expansion or developments, or reward performance and achievement. Profit is not earnings; they should be calculated as an overhead cost.

How to calculate profit margins

Be clear about what you mean as there is more than one type of profit.

How to work out gross profit

Your gross profit is your total sales minus your direct costs. Direct costs are the costs of making your product or selling your service. These include the costs of your raw materials, transportation of those materials, and employees' wages.

How to work out net profit

This is how much you've earned after you've subtracted your operating expenses from your profit, which include rent and business insurance. This is the one most small business monitor their performance on.

How to work out operating profit

Operating profit is your income from sales after deducting operating expenses (such as rent, equipment, and employee payroll). It also excludes things like taxes, interest, and profit or loss from investments. It also factors in non-cash expenses (depreciation of equipment).

Calculating operating profit can be a useful way to understand how efficient your business operations are before tax. It can also indicate whether you've got your pricing strategy right and how you're managing costs. A good accountant will help you get your head around what this means for your business and will help you.

To estimate average profit levels for your sector I have included the following table:

Market Sector	Average Gross Profit Margin	Average Net Profit Margin
Marketing	25%	1%
Building Materials	29%	5%
Hospitality	30%	6%
Retail (online)	40%	5%
Retail (General)	25%	3%
Healthcare products	56%	11%
Computer services	30%	4%
Consultancy Services	40%	10%

How to factor market value into your pricing structure

Understanding the value that you offer is crucial if you want to pitch your price right. Having completed a costing calculation and understanding if you are a basic, middle ground or luxury service in your sector, you need to ascertain the market value (price range in your sector). This involves looking at the levels of service offered by your competitors and seeing what they charge as a guideline.

Ideally, your prices should cover all your costs and overheads, there should be a percentage profit included, and should be in a range of similar services that share your sector position.

It is important to remember that your prices are not fixed, you can adjust them if they are not achieving what you need them to do.

Ultimately your price is governed by what people are willing to pay for your level of service. Once the price has been set it is important that your marketing activity explains the value that your customers get for that price and why they should use you rather than a competitor.

Having the right 'pricing' mindset

Often it is about believing that what you offer is value for money, so the psychology of buying is important. You need to understand your ideal client and exactly what problems you solve for them. This helps you to justify your prices to yourself, then to your market.

You are the expert on you; the quality you offer, and your unique selling points help you to accept your worth and therefore justify your prices.

Whilst it's important to be an individual in business and not just follow in the footsteps of others, pricing is one occasion when you need to know what others are doing. Unless your product is unique, you're in a shared marketplace and it's helpful to know what other people are charging.

Understanding market demand

The FreshBooks' US survey of women business owners 2022 gives insight into why they earn less than male business owners in the same industries.

Women entrepreneurs reported:

- 20% believe they must charge less than male equivalents to get and keep clients.
- 34% have experienced gender discrimination while self-employed.
- 30% believe they're not taken as seriously as their male peers.
- 30% believe they must work harder than men who do the same work.

There were some differences in terms of working hours and accommodating childcare for holidays, lower rates persist even when these are factored in. This strongly suggests that women provide a limiting barrier to their earning potential because of preconceived ideas and stereotyping.

All is not doom and gloom, however. There are several things' women can do to reverse this trend.

1. Connect with others. *"The women who were most confident about their pricing and self-value were regular networkers, particularly those who were members of a network group."* Positive reinforcement from other women entrepreneurs had a measured effect on the way they felt about their rates and services they offered.

2. Stress value over price. Business owners who find it easy to talk about the value they bring to their clients struggled less with the pricing dilemma.

3. Work on being more confident. Changing the mindset is crucial. If you understand your **'why'** and the value your clients receive from you, it is easier to differentiate between your offering and your competitors. You can then speak to clients with the confidence of conviction that you offer a value for money service.

4. Understand that there will always be people that cannot afford your service and that is because they are not your target market. The key is to fine-tune your marketing so that you accurately target those that have a need and can afford to use you.

Discounts and giveaways

Once you have established a pricing structure that you are happy with you may want to consider the issue of discounts and promotions. Discounts and promotions need to be calculated and offered on a very limited basis as part of an overall marketing campaign. Uncontrolled use will seriously damage the profitability of your business.

Three common pricing strategies are:

- **Bundling:** this is a technique to group products or services together and give a small discount to the client. This works because some of the overhead costs will be less on a single order rather than multiple orders and the overall client spend will be higher. Many businesses use bundling as an effective way to upsell to existing clients. This is particularly useful for product-based, MLM businesses.
- **Tiered services:** offer levels of services that specify a set of features and carry fixed prices for each tier. An example would be car valeting services offering bronze, silver, and gold washes.
- **Loss leaders or giveaways:** involve pricing some services for less than they cost to provide, in order to tempt clients to purchase and see what else you provide. Works mainly for online or physical retail businesses to help to 'get them through the door' and browse around.

There are lots of ways to price your products and services, but the most important thing is understanding how your pricing works and why it is critical to your profitability. Ultimately you are in charge, so your pricing is up to you. What you need to keep at the forefront of your mind is that you are paid what you are worth for a job well done. That should always be your starting point.

7: Your Personal Brand

By Sarah Gray

When we start a business, it is common place to spend a significant amount of time, energy, and money on our business brand. We all know multiple 'big brands' that have undoubtedly spent millions on developing a recognisable brand and we think that to be recognised we have to somehow follow suit - without the large budget! But how would you feel knowing that, in reality, we, as female business owners, already possess something that is equally as powerful and doesn't cost a fortune? It's called our Personal Brand. In this chapter, we will explore what a Personal Brand is, why we, as female business owners, need one, and crucially how we recognise and further develop our own.

What is a personal brand?

"A true personal brand revolves around what other people say about you."

*www.*personalbrand.com

"Your brand is what people say about you when you are not in the room."

Jeff Bezos. Amazon Founder

Your personal brand is the unique combination of skills, behaviour, personality, and values that make you who you are. It is how you present yourself to the world and consequently, to your prospective clients. The way you interact with people, how those people perceive you and your business, and how they emotionally connect with you and your business, is directly related to your personal brand.

You've probably heard the phrase *"people buy people"*. Don't underestimate how absolutely true this is. People will choose to do business with people they know, like and trust. It is a positive emotional connection between you as the business owner and your prospective client that is required in a strong personal brand. People want to do business with people who care, are passionate about what they do and who actually do what they say they are going to do. Ultimately, your personal brand is far more than a snazzy logo! A useful way to view a personal brand is by using the iceberg analogy - it's the visible stuff! But of course it's a lot more than just what you wear. Your personal brand comes across in the way you look, sound, and behave. For example, your tone of voice, your body language and charisma to name just a few. This doesn't mean that the foundations are not important. In fact they are a vital piece upon which to build your personal brand. Your values, strengths, aspirations, and such-like are not always visible to others but all of these elements need to be solid in order for you to show up with the strong visible elements such as your social skills, first impressions, etc.

The Importance of a Personal Brand for you and your business

"You never get a second chance to make a first impression."

Just as you might quickly judge a shop by its window display, so the first impression you make will be how your potential clients decide whether or not they wish to buy from you. Your personal brand is your shop window. It is your one chance to make that first impression. Building trust is key and your personal brand is the initial tool you can use to achieve this. When a dream client feels that they know you and gets a feel for how much value you offer, you are gaining their trust and strengthening the relationship even before they spend money with your business.

The ideal goal is for your business to be the one that your dream clients think of first when they need your product or service. In order to achieve this, your business needs to stand out, both in your industry and from your competitors.

How do you discover your personal brand?

Knowing that people buy people and those first impressions really do count, the best thing you can do is to become the face of your business and consistently make the very best impression you can. Now of course, for some, this is no problem and you'll relish the visibility. For others though, the thought of being so visible could fill you with dread and fear.

> *"People don't buy what you do; they buy why you do it. The goal is not to do business with everybody that needs what you have. The goal is to do business with people who believe what you believe."* **Simon Sinek**

Let us go back to the personal brand iceberg. Every moment you can spend working on knowing your values and beliefs is hugely valuable. When you are thinking of your values, dig deep. Just saying, "I'm professional" isn't enough. This is very important but as a business owner, being professional should be a given. By digging deeper you will find more values and beliefs that set you apart from your competition and subsequently will resonate with your ideal client.

Can you remember why you went into business in the first place? It is important to know this. Why? Because knowing this enables you to write your story. You might think your story is nothing special, boring even, but told well, your story is what will attract your dream client. So use your story as the foundation for your personal brand.

Whenever and however you show up, be it online in a video, or offline in an email, you must be authentically you. Avoid writing or presenting in a way you've seen someone else do, because that won't be your voice. Avoid thinking that any video you do has to be scripted and perfect because again, that isn't getting your personality across. Of course, write bullet points on what to talk about but try to use your own natural conversational style which will be full of your passion and be truly authentic which in turn will give your potential clients an insight into the real you.

One element of personal branding that often prevents female business owners from confidently being the face of their business, is the indecision around what to wear. The internal dialogue around what she thinks she 'should' wear and fear that in those all-important first few seconds of a first impression, clothes do a lot of the talking before you do can stop her in her tracks.

The advice here is to work on your personal style. As previously mentioned, it is not the only element of your personal brand but it is an important one and can easily be addressed after you have the solid foundations in your personal brand iceberg.

Your clothing needs to:

- reflect your personal and business brand values
- complement your personality
- complement your colouring and figure
- be appropriate
- be current
- give you confidence.

Ultimately, know who you are, know how to tell your story, know your values and beliefs, know who your dream client is, and be consistent in showing up both on and offline so you attract the attention of those dream clients.

8: How to Stand Out in a Crowded Marketplace

By Helen Chidgey

A s a business owner it's of paramount importance that you consider where you sit within your relevant industry in comparison to all your competitors so that you can ensure that you are seen, your message is heard and that your customers can find you.

As an ambassador with a leading brand of skin care sold on a party-plan basis, I am well placed to offer some insight into this important topic and to highlight areas I've had to consider when building my business from scratch to what has become a full-time, lucrative, enjoyable, and successful career. I sit within an industry that is valued at £26.7 billion for the year ending 2022 according to Companies House, and as an Ambassador for Tropic Skincare, I also stand shoulder-to-shoulder with 20,000 other ambassadors all looking to find, nurture, and delight their customers.

The aim of this chapter is to give you some key areas to focus your attention on when you're looking at ways to make sure you and your business stand out from the crowd in whatever industry you find yourself. I have an acronym to share with you which may sound a little strange! By way of explanation may I say that when I first started out in business, I felt a little uncomfortable and somewhat overexposed. Similar to how I feel when wearing a certain shape of underwear - maybe they work for you, but I just can't wear a thong, no thank you, they are not for me! So, the acronym I wish to share with you is PANTS.

In the early days as a naive newly registered Ambassador, I was definitely out of my comfort zone and had to work on strategies to help me through various situations that ultimately shaped the businessperson I am today. These experiences have informed the tips I'm about to share with you and I hope through digesting these tips you'll feel a little more certain about how you can stand out from the crowd in a positive way that aligns with you and your core values.

Personal branding

First of all, let us consider your personal branding. This is a large topic in itself and has already seen some exposure in the personal styling chapter.

Personal branding is all about building relationships smoothly and effectively to make sure potential customers understand you and what you have to offer.

You'll want to consider a number of areas. For example:

- How memorable are you to others and why (let's make sure it's for all the right reasons)?

- How well do you connect with those around you?

- Do you connect on an emotional level?

- Do you give good eye contact both online and in person?

- Is your body language open and welcoming?

- Do you make a great first impression on someone? (Don't forget the last impression you make is important too!)

- How do you represent yourself?

- Is there a certain look your profession favours?

- Can you add your own signature version to this look or can you dress in an outlandish way that will be truly memorable without crossing any professional boundaries?

- How do you make people feel so they will remember you long after meeting you?

Relationship-building is so important to build that magical '***know, like and trust***' effect that is crucial to your success. You also need to consider what printed branding you choose. Perhaps you are affiliated with a large organisation that employs specialists to design your marketing materials, so all the hard work is done for you. What else can you do to make sure you are known as you, not just another representative of that company? If you are your own designer, carefully consider the use of fonts, colour choices and logos so that they all reflect your own values and the theme of your product or service.

Attraction

One of the keys to success is attracting those people that are ready to become your customers, who in essence share your values and have problems that you can solve. To do this will mean sharing your own story, how you've come to where you are now, what started your journey and your over-arching WHY you are in business. By sharing this with authenticity, people can clearly see whether they are drawn to you as a person first and foremost, and secondly whether your business is a match for their needs. It may not be immediately but that doesn't mean it will never happen, keep yourself fresh in their minds and over time they may be more ready to engage with you. You will notice that your WHY has become a common thread throughout many of the chapters in this book.

Networking

Many entrepreneurs take part in networking and there are many official groups in person and online where networking meetings take place. In truth, networking can be part of your everyday lives. It's that chat at the pub, the conversation at the bus stop or a catch up on the school run - all these provide the opportunity to network. All these situations allow moments where you may be able to share your story and connect with others, building relationships as you go about your daily life.

More formal networking events, however, are a brilliant way to meet like-minded individuals who may be your ideal client or lead you to connect with your ideal clients. They offer chances to collaborate with others, for you to gain new skills, to build confidence and at some stage find and engage with your ideal clients.

Having some sort of networking strategy is your key to success in the networking world. Think carefully about your potential audience and whether your ideal client will hang out in a certain group before committing to an expensive membership. You want to maintain a good return on any time and money you invest in networking. Most groups offer an opportunity to get a feel for the group before you sign up, they do vary considerably in the way they operate so make sure you love it before joining! Each networking group has its own format but definitely go along fully prepared. More than likely, you'll need to have an introductory 'pitch' to share with the group so make sure you have this ready and that you feel comfortable with delivering it. Most meeting facilitators will coach you on the format that is expected but generally it's NOT about selling your products/services but more about raising curiosity about what you do so sharing customer testimonials, problems you've solved, or a case study will help you build a rapport with the individuals in the room. Sell the sizzle not the sausage as my dad used to say!

Learn more about networking and how to ensure you get a return on your investment in upcoming chapters.

Training and knowledge

This section is all about bolstering that all important 'know, like and trust' factor, particularly the trust element. As business owners, it's important to be seen as the expert in your field, whatever industry you may be in. Wherever possible make sure you take advantage of any opportunities to improve your personal knowledge and update your qualifications. After all, if we can keep learning and growing ourselves, surely, we will have higher self-esteem and feel more enriched as a result. Furthermore, don't be afraid to ask for help, being able to reach out to others is a strength. Seeing us step outside our comfort zone will further validate that we have a desire to be recognised as that genuine expert that people will turn to when the need arises.

Show up and shine

Showing up at industry-related events will help raise your profile as will entering business awards. The latter in particular is a wonderful way to evaluate your business and where you've come from, review what you've achieved and identify any areas for growth, and should you be a winner there's another trophy in your cabinet that cements you as the expert in your field.

You've got great skills, you're a fount of knowledge, you're a star in your area, you've got a story to share, and people need you. These are the thoughts you need to fill your mind with at every opportunity. We're talking about having a positive mindset that chases away the negative thoughts, and a sprinkle of self-belief goes a long way in helping others connect with you. Have a clear goal in mind that makes you want to leap out of bed in the morning, and that drives you along the road to success.

With that in mind, it's time to show up and shine. Be around others as your authentic self, brimming with enthusiasm for what you do. Your products or service are irresistible!

Hopefully, with these tips in mind, you can find your positive PANTS that will ensure you truly do stand out from the crowd.

9: Premises That Work for You

By Nina Molyneux

In my therapy business, when I started out, I thought carefully about whether to work from home (lots of therapists do, and it's reassuringly cheap) or whether to find somewhere else. I realised that I really didn't want to share my home with clients for several reasons: I had children and I didn't want them to feel constrained to be quiet if they were at home when I was working; home is a sacred, personal space for me and I didn't want to compromise on the sense of safety that I have in it by opening it up to clients rather than friends and family; I'm not very tidy at home, and I really didn't want to have to become so for the benefit of clients! These were all good reasons from my personal perspective, and I also felt that from a client's point of view my bodywork practice would come across as something to be taken more seriously if I had professional premises. At the same time, I didn't want a big, fixed overhead when I was starting out. I really was setting up with nothing but my skills and time.

With all that in mind, I managed to find various premises over the years, mainly on a pay-as-you-go basis which meant I never got caught out with rent that I couldn't pay. If I wasn't seeing clients, I wasn't paying rent, which was a big bonus, especially as I worked less during the school holidays while my children were young. Much to my surprise, somewhere always came up when I needed it and I managed to negotiate flexible terms with remarkably little difficulty. Not surprisingly, some worked better than others. Aside from the practicalities of the facilities available, the most successful places were the ones where the balance between personal and professional, that I like to strike in my work, was shared by the business I was renting from. Basically, the atmosphere was right, which mattered hugely to me, and in the way clients perceived me.

With time, my business grew, and I was seeing clients Monday to Friday. I ended up working in three different locations, no two days consecutively, so that every day I lugged my kit somewhere different, moved the furniture so the layout of the room was right for my purposes, saw clients, then packed everything up again before putting everything back to where I'd found it. It was exhausting both physically and mentally because I was constantly on the move, carrying equipment, and creating the atmosphere I wanted for my clients in places that weren't mine. At the same time, it was a little disorienting for clients who had to be clear about where to find me if their appointments fell on different days during a course of treatment. I was aware of those difficulties, but I was continuing to work on the assumption that a fixed overhead was a dangerous thing. Then at the end of one financial year, I looked with fresh eyes at the amount of rent I had paid over twelve months, and I was shocked. It finally made me question my pay-as-you-go approach, and I investigated how much it would cost me to rent somewhere full time. When I looked into it, I realised that even with utility bills, I'd be paying no more than I already was, and I'd have all the advantages of being settled somewhere and being able to set things up as I wanted them.

With all the experience built up over ten years working in lots of different places I had a clear idea of what I liked and didn't like in a premises. I drew the layout of my ideal setup, including aspects of the outside appearance, so that the welcome clients received began before they'd even set foot in the building. Armed with my list of requirements and desires, I looked around and was disappointed with what I saw. The budget wasn't the problem. It was more a case of the types of premises that were around. I knew what the most important features were, though, and I stuck to my guns, looking at places, building relationships with local landlords, and getting a feel for the market. It was so tempting to compromise on location and the features that were important to me yet difficult to find, but I was clear about what was a requirement for me and what was a nice-to-have.

After eighteen months, I heard of a property that would become available in the location I wanted. It was residential, a tiny flat, but it ticked all my high priority boxes. I knew the landlady because I'd had various conversations with her over the last year and a half, so I called her and asked about it before it had been advertised. The upshot of it all is that I secured the premises, the landlady made a successful application to the council for change-of-use planning permission and made a few adjustments to the fittings in the flat so that it served my purpose pretty much to perfection. And all for a sensible, affordable rent. Those premises transformed my daily experience of arriving at work to one of settled ease. I arrive in the mornings knowing that everything is already set up for the start of my day, because it will be as I left it the day before. I have complete freedom in arranging appointments because I have no need to co-ordinate with another therapist or landlord if it's slightly outside my normal hours. The extra responsibilities of renting full time are well worth the freedom I gain from having full time access. I love it, my clients love it, and it's become part of my brand.

Some of the things I learnt along the way

1. It's tempting to compromise on important personal boundaries when setting up a business, thinking that sacrifices are necessary to get a new venture off the ground. That may be true, but if you don't leave enough space for your personal comfort, you won't be able to keep going when things are tough. For me, that was manifest in the decision not to see clients at home, and it was worth every penny of rent that I have since paid to preserve my privacy. Whatever your personal no-go areas are, it's worth protecting them.

2. It's surprising what rental terms you can come to if you are clear about what you want, even if you don't think negotiation is your thing.

3. Choosing premises is about more than the practical facilities they provide – if you're sharing a room or a building, you're effectively associating yourself with the other people and organisations in it, and that feeds into the atmosphere you work in and the impression you give to employees, customers, and suppliers.

4. It's good to keep reviewing assumptions and fears. Things change and what served me well at the beginning did not serve me well after a while. I was busy being stoic, as so many of us are, without questioning the necessity of renting space in a piecemeal fashion. I could have made the shift and enjoyed the benefits of my own premises a lot sooner if I'd been more open-minded.

5. Being clear about what I was looking for, whether that be flexibility of terms, location or physical features of the premises was key in finding good places to work. With my longer-term premises, it meant I waited for and got what I needed and wanted rather than rushing into somewhere that was ok but not great.

6. Building a relationship with property owners and letting my contacts in general know what I was looking for meant that I found out about the perfect place before it was openly on the market, and the landlady really put herself out for me to make the changes I needed. Without the previous contact to set the scene, I'm pretty sure that my beautiful therapy space would still be a tiny residential property, and I would have missed out on the happy years I have spent working in it.

10: Technology for Business

By Ellen Badat

A few years ago, I was in a yoga class and the teacher was walking around checking the students' postures, she came over to me, looked at my form and whispered in my ear, "I have never met anyone who can cheat at yoga, until today." I smiled and said, "The path of least resistance."

For me, the phrase means keeping it simple and finding the best way to achieve my goal that works for me. The emphasis here being 'works for me' - more about this later.

Keeping it simple, not only applies to the way I live my life but also to my business, and especially when it comes to technology! I like technology, I can see the benefits of what it can do, but I can also see the dangers. I am not just referring to computer viruses, malware, and other malicious activities, but the way it can cause isolation and distraction in everyday life.

Almost every business in the world uses technology in some way, for most it is for the general running of their business, communication with customers and suppliers, social media, record-keeping, the list goes on. There are so many choices for business owners to choose from, desktop computer or laptop, which operating system, Windows, or Apple Mac, which phone, Android or iPhone, printers, scanners, separate devices, or an all-in-one?

This is when 'keep it simple' and 'what works for me' apply.

Question: Desktop or laptop?

- Do you have a dedicated workspace or a fixed desk to work at?
- Do you have the space for a computer tower?
- Do you need to take the device with you to see clients?

- Do you want the flexibility of working from multiple places i.e., at your desk, in the garden, a coffee shop, a co-working space, your client's premises?

- Do you need the processing speed of a powerful computer?

- Do you want to have a large screen/monitor to use if you are going to be spending a long time looking at it?

All these points will help you decide whether you go for a desktop or a laptop. Answer the point which is most relevant first. If taking a device with you when you go and see clients is a must or being able to work from multiple locations, then a laptop is the obvious choice. If you do have a fixed desk to work at and you want a large screen with separate keyboard and mouse, then you can get a docking station for the laptop. Depending on the model, a docking station allows you to leave the monitor, keyboard, mouse, printer etc connected, and when you are at your desk you connect the laptop to the docking station, and you can use the large monitor etc. When you want to take the laptop with you, you just unplug the laptop from the docking station to work in a new location.

Personally, I have had laptops for the past 10 years, however, earlier this year, I was looking at replacing it. Whilst looking for a replacement and asking myself whether a laptop really suited my needs and working method, I decided to get a desktop computer. I have the space for it and have a dedicated working area, I already had a large screen, wireless keyboard, and mouse that the new desktop computer could connect to, and I rarely visit clients. The overall decider for me was that I wanted a more powerful computer, I want to be able to easily add more storage, to add a high-end dedicated graphics card, so when I am editing photos, I can do so easily. I still have my laptop in reserve, so if I do want to work in the garden, a coffee shop, or when I am on holiday, I have it with me.

Question: Windows or Mac? Android or iOS?

This comes down to personal choice. My advice when speaking to clients is to go with what you know. If you have always used a Windows computer, then I would recommend sticking with Windows. If you have always used or are familiar with the Mac operating system, then go with a Mac.

The same with your mobile phone, what are you used to? Android or iPhone? Unless you particularly want to learn a new operating system for the computer or mobile, then stick with what you know. Do not feel pressured into buying a computer/mobile that you are not comfortable with - use the 'what works for me' method. Your clients are working with you, because of what you do and can provide for them, so whether you use Windows or Mac, Android, or iPhone, it should not be relevant to how you achieve the goal and complete the job for the client.

I currently use a Windows desktop computer and an iPhone. I have used Windows for over 25 years, and I am very familiar with it. I have had, and can use a Mac, but my preference is Windows. The same with my mobile phone, I have had an Android phone in the past, but I prefer an iPhone; this is the setup that 'works for me'.

Question: What domain name do I register?

Your domain name is the address of your business on the internet, usually it will also be part of your email address. So my business domain is purpletree.solutions and my email is ellen@purpletree.solutions.

There are many different domain extensions you can register. There are the standard .co.uk and .com, also .uk, .net, .photography, and of course .solutions, plus many, many more. It can be tempting to register lots of different extensions when you are setting up your business or even rebranding, but remember these all have a financial cost, and you generally only use one as your main domain. I will add here, it can make sense to register the main extensions to protect your brand, so .co.uk, .uk, and .com. This depends on where you live and operate your business, so for example, a Canadian-based business, would want to register the .ca extension, and any local variations for their area. It is good if your domain name includes what you do, so if you are an accountant, try and include it in the name, but also try not to make the domain name too long. This is where using an alternative domain extension can help, so for example, purpletree.solutions v's purpletreesolutions.co.uk

Question: Which email system?

There are numerous types of email systems available, Microsoft Exchange, Google Mail, POP, IMAP, service provider-hosted, in-house-hosted systems. The two biggest ones are Microsoft Exchange (or Microsoft 365) and Google Mail, which are both paid-for systems. Again, it comes back to what works for you. My personal preference is Microsoft Exchange which is part of the Microsoft 365 system. I have been using Exchange for many years and I understand its functionality and the way it deals with emails, my calendar, contacts, tasks, and notes.

The Google system works differently, but again, it comes back to what you know. If you are used to a particular system, it makes sense to stick with it. You may consider changing or adding a second mail system if you are working with colleagues or clients who use a different system, where it makes sense for everyone to be using the same system.

Question: What about a website?

The biggest question here is, "What do you want your website to achieve?"

- Are you looking to just have a presence, or a portfolio of work and the services you offer?
- Are you selling products or services directly on the website?

The answers to these questions will help point you in the right direction for your website. There are multiple ways to achieve each of these options, with template systems such as SquareSpace, Wix, and Shopify. There is WordPress which can be hosted on almost any web server, or custom-built websites where the designer writes the code for the site. All of these types of sites can be configured to be a presence for your business, all the way to a full e-commerce system for selling online.

There are pros and cons for each option.

Hosted template systems like SquareSpace and Wix provide you with a user-friendly portal to update and make changes to your website. Generally, you will find lots of help files or videos explaining how to carry out tasks, make updates etc. Some systems also include an SSL certificate for the site as standard and the host will maintain the template and server to keep it as secure as possible. The downside is that you are then locked into their system, which means you cannot design the site on their system and then move it to another website host.

With WordPress, which uses a system called Themes, and custom code sites, the portal is not as straightforward, if there is one at all, as you may need to edit code to make updates. The benefit is that you generally have a lot more control over the layout of the pages as you are not conforming to a template as such. Also, these types of sites can usually be hosted on any webserver. If you decide to have a WordPress or custom site built with code, then I highly recommend that you take a support package with the designer to make sure the site is maintained and kept up to date.

Question: What other tech stuff do I need to think about?

There are a few other areas which are important when you consider the tech and the systems you use in your business.

Security – there are numerous products on the market for computer and device security. Generally, they all do the same job, and it comes down to personal preference. I use a business level product and it has additional features and options that many standard products do not.

Password management software - is also highly recommended. This allows you to store all your passwords in a safe place and you have to remember one password to access the password manager.

As with any security on a device, it is only as secure as the password and the person using it, if the password is your pet's name and house number, there is a much higher chance someone will guess it, rather than a randomly-generated password, which yes, to start with, is difficult to remember, but once you have entered it a few times, it will become second nature to you.

File storage – some email systems like Microsoft 365 and Google Mail also come with file storage options, which give you space on one of their servers for you to store files. Microsoft 365 comes with OneDrive and SharePoint. These serve two different functions depending on what you are looking to do with files and how you want them to be stored and used.

How you store your files for your business, depends on what you do and how you work. If you are using an online accounting system, you can upload expenses and receipts to the system, and they are stored in your accounts. If you are working with confidential or sensitive information, you may not want to store the data in a general online system, but rather opt for a specialist online package designed to hold sensitive information, or to keep paper records instead.

My suggestion is to plan out what information you will be storing, which will point you in the right direction of where to store your data. I keep electronic copies of all my expenses and the invoices sent to clients. As much as I use technology, I also know what it is like when it goes wrong!

Backups – clients ask me what should I back up and how?

The answer to what you should back up is what would cause you the most problems or upset if you no longer had those files. If you lost all your business files, records of customers, transactions, quotations, etc., this would cause you problems when having to answer client questions or providing them a product or service. If you were to lose more personal files, like photographs of family, holidays, special occasions, it would be upsetting as there is a good chance you will not be able to recreate them.

For a local backup that you do yourself on to an external storage drive or USB stick, it can be as simple as copying the files across. You need to make sure the drive is then stored safely and securely. The biggest problem with this method is if something happened to your computer or laptop and the backup device at the same time. For example, if you are working from a home office and there was a fire or flood and the computer, and the backup drive were both damaged beyond repair, you have lost all of your data.

There are numerous online backup systems, which can automatically backup your data to a secure and encrypted data storage area. Some of these will connect into your Microsoft 365 or Google system at the server level and do a backup of your email and documents, so they are stored separately to the main cloud files. This becomes very important if you were to be subject to ransomware, which means the files on the computer are encrypted and you would need to pay to get them back. Whereas having the third-party automated backup means you can restore the files from the last known good copy after you have had your computer system checked for problems and any infections.

Summary

There are many areas to the tech available to businesses, plus the different combinations of systems you can use. The things to keep in mind are, keep it simple and ask yourself, "Does this work for me?" If it is too complicated or does not suit your way of working, chances are you will not use it and get frustrated in the process. I remember walking into a client's office and the two main staff were having a heated discussion about a project they were working on. The one said to the other, *"It's not rocket-science."* The second person looked at the first, thought about it for a moment and said, *"Actually it is."* They were both nuclear engineers, designing a part for a nuclear reactor.

So, remember, for most people, it is not rocket-science, keep it simple and ask, "Does this work for me?"

11: Multi-Level Marketing

By Vicky Farmer

Have you heard of multi-level marketing? And if you have, do you have a positive or a negative impression of it?

Essentially it is a business model that enables people to set up their own business with very low start-up costs, great flexibility, generous rates of commission and a culture of carrot over stick i.e., successes are rewarded as opposed to poor performance being punished. It also provides opportunities for good quality training in business, sales, and personal development at very low cost or even free. And there is usually a network of people in the background willing you on and helping you to succeed by sharing the benefit of their experience.

It sounds great. In fact, it sounds too good to be true, so what's the catch? Speaking from my own personal experience – and I have worked in multi-level marketing for over 13 years – I still haven't found the catch. What I have found is that if you treat it as a business and work hard ("It's flexible not optional," as one of my mentors used to say) you will reap the rewards. So why is it sometimes viewed in a bad light? Very often social media groups aimed at creating community groups to provide support for small businesspeople will operate a blanket ban on multi-level marketing businesses, selling groups will ban multi-level marketing businesses from taking part in their events and markets, and if I had £1 for every time I was asked if my business was a "Pyramid Scheme" I'd never have to work again.

Let's have a look at what we mean by multi-level marketing and hopefully it will help to demystify some of the myths that appear to exist around this way of running a business, especially when we realise that many household brand names operate through this type of business model and globally in 2020, the industry reported sales of $189.6 billion with over 124 million people operating as independent consultants. (Source: Zippa. November 2022)

What is it?

Multi-level marketing (MLM) is also known as network marketing, referral marketing, direct selling, or social selling. It's a method of selling products direct from the manufacturer to the public using sales representatives rather than retail outlets. This way it dispenses with the need for wholesalers and retailers within the supply chain, which can help to keep costs down. If you've ever bought products from companies like Avon, Tropic Skincare, Usbourne Books or Herbalife International Inc, these are MLM companies. And the ultimate MLM that everyone must have heard of – Tupperware.

How does it work?

The sales force are not employees of the company. Instead, they work as independent consultants. There is usually a start-up cost. Earnings are based on commissions resulting from sales and recruiting new team members who you would be responsible for training. Imagine being the owner of your own business where you build a network of customers and team members, and earn commission based on the sales of yourself and your team.

The Compensation Plan

This is how the reward structure is referred to. The general format is similar from one MLM to another although the details will vary. This could involve differences in the start-up cost, the commission rates on sales by you and your team members, the value of additional rewards provided, and the commission and other remuneration given for sharing the business opportunity with other people.

What are the advantages?

- It's a very easy way to get started in business. When starting your own business, it can take large amounts of capital, but with MLM, the start-up costs are relatively low to acquire a basic starter kit.

- It isn't necessary to hold stock as the company will ship orders directly to customers. This is beneficial as there is minimal need for storage space and no need to invest financially in stock.

- It is a very flexible way of working. You can choose your hours, choose when and where you work, have a good work-life balance, be there when the family needs you and never miss a parent's evening or school play again.

- Flexibility extends to the way of working. You get to choose whether you work online, including through social media, or face to face, whether you meet customers one-to-one, or do group demos. The options are endless, and the choice is yours.

- Marketing materials, branded items and even a personalised website, are supplied by the company at relatively low cost. This represents a great saving compared to setting up an independent business from scratch where it can feel like a bottomless pit of money is required to create bespoke branding and marketing.

- The key to success with MLM businesses is good communication because a lot of business is done by word of mouth. Therefore, communication skills are really important and one of the pros of an MLM business is to help you build these skills by providing good quality training and personal development for free or at very low cost.

- All businesses have to face rejection, but MLM businesses seem to face more than their fair share of negativity. So in this business, you are taught to deal with rejection very well. As a result, you become more resilient, and this is a valuable trait to have in any business. Having the capacity to face rejection head-on and deal with it creates a successful businessperson in any sector.

- Because MLM independent consultants are not employees of the companies whose brands they represent, there is a culture of motivation through incentivising. In other words, there are no mandatory targets and no penalties for poor performance, but instead incentives are provided for making a positive contribution. This could take the form of free products, cash bonuses, free luxury holidays and other benefits that are worth going the extra mile to achieve. Very much a carrot rather than a stick approach.

- Depending on the type of product being marketed, it can be possible to start earning very quickly and develop a passive income stream, which is useful for developing multiple income streams (see Chapter 5).

- Being your own boss. Although you are working with a particular brand with specific policies and procedures, you have the freedom to work how you wish within those parameters. It's a bit like a franchise where you have the safety net of an established brand but unlike a franchise, you have more freedom to operate in a way that suits you and you don't usually have to work within a set territory. So, although you are in business on your own, you are not alone, as you will have trainers and mentors within the business to guide you to be successful.

What are the disadvantages?

- Not everyone who joins an MLM company becomes rich and successful. This is largely dependent on the mindset of the individual because at the end of the day, everyone starts with the same kit, and it just depends on what they do with it.

- Being part of an MLM requires you to be self-employed which some people may not fancy. It means finding your own customers and dealing with your own accounts and tax. And of course, there is no job security in the conventional sense and no guaranteed income. This is not for everyone.

- It's a marathon not a sprint and it can take a long time to grow an MLM business. Some people are impatient and not prepared to invest the time or deal with rejection and this may account for the fact that 50% of participants drop out after a year and only 25% are reported to turn a profit. (Source: Fundera October 2022)

- It's a Pyramid Scheme! This warrants a section on its own as it is probably the most frequently repeated myth about MLM and I am sure that most people who say it, have no idea what a Pyramid Scheme actually is.

It's a Pyramid Scheme!

First of all, I need to say – Pyramid Schemes are illegal. They became illegal in the UK in 2008 under the Consumer Protection from Unfair Trading Regulations and anyone operating one can be prosecuted. Similar legislation exists in other countries around the world so if MLMs are

Pyramid Schemes and therefore illegal, how do they manage to attract over 124 million people generating nearly $190 billion in revenues per year?

A Pyramid Scheme involves an unsustainable business which rewards people for enrolling others into a business that offers a non-existent product. Members are recruited to a scheme in exchange for a joining fee, with the promise of payments for recruiting more people into the scheme. These payments come from a proportion of the amounts received from the people they recruit. As recruiting multiplies, the maths alone makes it clear that most members will be unable to profit because the number of recruits needed to make it work becomes unsustainable, which is why such schemes were made illegal as recently as 2008.

The Pyramid Scheme label comes in because these schemes tended to start with one person at the top of the pyramid and the structure gets wider, like a pyramid, as each layer tries to recruit more people to the scheme. In theory the money generated at the bottom (the widest part) of the structure from more people paying to join in, then flows up through the layers so those at the top, cream off the most. But, if you think about any organisation from a trading company to a church, to the armed forces, and of course an MLM business, isn't that how they all operate? The people lower down the pyramid do most of the work to generate income that flows up through the pyramid structure to the CEO at the top who has the highest salary and the massive bonus. Does that make every limited company in the UK an illegal pyramid scheme? Of course not!

The main difference between a Pyramid Scheme (the illegal type) and a legitimate trading company, is that the structure and payments flowing through it do not incorporate the sale of products. People operating within an MLM pay to join, which may be where the confusion arises, but it's usually a relatively low amount and represents a starter kit of products at a heavily discounted price, to help get started with having products to demonstrate. After that the emphasis is very much on selling products in exchange for commission, and by sponsoring other independent consultants to join the business, additional amounts can be earned by the sponsoring consultant (often referred to as override commissions) based on their recruit's sales. However, the payments come direct from the company, not from the consultants themselves and just like any other business, no-one in an MLM has to pay another person in the organisation in exchange for the promise of receiving remuneration.

In other words, an MLM is just a means of organising the way a company operates, that makes it easy for the overarching company (which has no workforce and associated costs, and minimal overheads), and also provides a simple way for people to have their own business (flexibility, low start-up costs, free/low-cost training, and support). And it is definitely NOT a Pyramid Scheme. So where does that leave us?

Are you ready to give it a try?

Here are some top tips to have a successful experience with an MLM:

- There are many to choose from, so pick a product that you are passionate about, and it will be much easier to sell.

- Be a product of the product – make sure you know the product range inside out so that when a customer asks about it, you can speak from personal experience. Remember 'facts tell, stories sell'.

- Work hard. MLM is a simple business model, but it's simple, not optional.

- Take advantage of all the training and support offered to you. This is an area first rate MLMs will have well in hand and it's generally free or very low cost compared with what you would expect to pay for a similar, commercially-available course.

- Be consistent if you want to build a successful business.

And if you are a customer of someone who operates an MLM business, remember – when you buy from a small business, an actual person does a little happy dance!

12: Why I Started My Multi-Level Marketing (MLM) Business

By Nicky Tonks

"Whatever you vividly imagine, ardently desire, sincerely believe, and enthusiastically act upon must inevitably come to pass!"

Paul J. Meyer - Founder LMI Inc.

Enthusiastic to be around for my husband's leadership development and coaching business, and take on his administration and accounts, I needed to give up my paid employment and find a part time job that not only provided an income, but one I felt passionate about, Utility Warehouse ticked all the boxes for me.

I have been a Partner for a few years, but life has got in the way on a few occasions over the years, which has meant I have not been as active as I would have liked, partly due to a lack of confidence, raising children, and being away from the workplace for a long time. Even though I had periods of inactivity I have never walked away from it completely, and it has always been on the back burner ready to fire up when the time was right again.

The company has evolved over the years and is now a simple model to follow, and to duplicate. It is much easier to see the rewards of your work sooner, so if you have big goals you want to reach it is a perfect business to be part of.

If you are analytical and prone to procrastinate and someone who looks for perfection, then you need to put it all to one side. Having a need-to-know attitude can be a good thing and helpful at times for the customer who likes to know the small detail, but do not let this attitude distract you from the main objective which is to speak to people and show them how you can help and ultimately build a team of like-minded people. Do not try to change what already works. There is a system to follow so don't try to change it, add to it, or think you know a better way, because you will waste time. Do what it says on the tin. Always remember you are a 'business owner'. Do not think of it as a little part-time job on the side. It is your new business that will take you to your future success, the vehicle to help turn dreams into reality.

Don't listen to the party poopers and the killjoys

There will be people you know that will dismiss your new venture, and will most likely be family and close friends, probably with a host of negative comments like, "Oh! Not one of those pyramid schemes." They will be the hardest nuts to crack and believe me, there are still some close to me who will not entertain it to this very day. Do not waste time trying to explain it to them, because once they see your success, they will be asking you how you do it.

Always associate with successful people in the business, as they want you to succeed, and being in their company will excite you, and fill you with the enthusiasm needed to be active every day, week, and month. Associate with positive, smiley happy people, within and outside of the business. Become one of them, become a leader.

Get comfortable being uncomfortable by networking

Networking is essential and it comes in all shapes and sizes. If you are new to the networking scene then take a deep breath and don't be afraid to jump straight in, there is a whole chapter dedicated to it in this book! There will be the option of face-to-face groups and virtual meetings. Visit groups more than once to get a feel for the people in the room. Most groups will allow at least two visits and some three, so you can then make your decision as to whether it's the right one for you. There are some expensive networking groups out there, but you don't have to spend a fortune. Look for groups that will genuinely want to help and support you, not just for prospecting, but for the knowledge and support the other business owners can give you. Do your best to come away with at least two 1-2-1 appointments in your diary.

Circumstances change

Circumstances change and life gets in the way, but even if you find you cannot devote as much time as you would like to the business, always do what is possible for you in your current situation. Adapting to change is crucial. Some changes are out of our control, so be ready to cope with a sudden change by making sure you have, daily, weekly, and monthly goals written down, with a target goal for each day. A current goal might not be the right one when a change occurs, so having other goals written and ready to work on is so important and keeps you focused on your business, making it easier to ride the storm of change.

An essential book for MLM business owners is '*The One Thing*' by Gary Keller. Keeping focused on the one thing you must do each day will give you the results you need to grow your business. If you have little time, choose the one thing you can do each day that will have the greatest impact on your business.

Personal development

Being part of an MLM business is a fantastic opportunity for personal development. Take part in the training, listen, and ask questions of other successful partners who will encourage and support you by showing you the tried and tested methods to help you create your own successful business. Find a way that suits you, and the time you have, to dedicate to your new venture. Don't forget you are now a business owner. Work on your business regularly, attend events as they are the best place to meet and speak with successful partners in the business. The ones just starting out and the partners who have been around for a few years can all help you on your journey.

Attending all the MLM events is a real positivity boost, and the recognition is so uplifting, you will want to experience it. Find a mentor. This could be the person who introduced you to the business. It could be someone who has joined your team, especially when you are both new to the business you can help and support each other and grow together, and new team members will see how you work and will want to be a part of it. Read personal development books relevant to your MLM business; any book that will increase your knowledge about yourself and your business.

Organise daily - create a structure to your day

Take 10 minutes at the start of every day to plan and prioritise your activities.

- Prioritise - Do the one thing that will get you the appointments and presentations and build your team. Touch your business every day in some way.
- Schedule blocks of time for your daily tasks
- Find a system for planning your daily activities and monthly goals
- Plan each step to reaching your goal, by tracking your progress daily, visualising and recording accomplishments
- Close each day by recording your accomplishments and always track your progress
- At the end of each day move any outstanding tasks to the following day
- Learn to say NO to interruptions

Marketing and social media

Multi-level businesses have their own structure for marketing their products and services. There are rules and regulations regarding the types of marketing allowed. Market yourself, tell your story and the stories of the people you have helped. Share why you started the business, how it has helped you and your family, and how you can help others do the same. The beauty of working with a multi-level business is the access to a multitude of resources, experts, and assistance. Marketing materials provided for you save time and allow you to add your own twist while following tried and tested methods. Networking is essential for marketing your business. Get to know your fellow networkers, help them understand what it is you do and how you can help, and become the person they can trust to refer to their friends, family, colleagues, and neighbours. A word of warning from personal experience: do not spread yourself too thinly across all the social media sites. Find the one or two sites where your ideal client/potential new customer spends their time.

Adapting to change

"Change is the law of life. And those who look only to the past or the present are certain to miss the future." – John F Kennedy

Circumstances change and life gets in the way for many reasons; a crisis occurs, our own choices, or life just happens.

Change can be a good thing. It sets us new challenges and when confronted with these challenges it makes us grow and more opportunities drop into our path. Embrace the changes and challenges, go back to your written plan and goals, give them a tweak, and remember your purpose, the reason WHY you set out on this journey.

Ride the wave of change and arrive on the beach a little battered but know where you are heading fully prepared to ride the next wave. Know that even if you cannot devote the time you would like to your business, it will always be there to pick up when you can devote more of your time once again. Do what is possible, for you, in your current circumstances. Don't check out completely. Check in and keep abreast of the changes happening within the business.

I wish you success on whichever road to you decide to take. Just remember it is your journey and only you can make it happen.

"You can have everything you want in life if you just help enough people to get what they want." –

Jim Rohn

13: Accounting & Bookkeeping

By Sue Green and Lorraine Willis

Bookkeeping in simple terms is keeping good records of your sales income and the expenses for your business. In this chapter we will share with you all the reasons why meticulous records are so important:

Record-keeping complies with the law

Good record-keeping is a legal requirement under the rules of assessment. Complying with HMRC requirements is in fact a very important reason why you should keep good records.

Manage your business and make it grow

If you don't have good records, it's much harder to make good business decisions and grow. By taking control and keeping excellent bookkeeping records, it will enable you to have a clear picture of your business and its financial status.

Keep up to date when dealing with customers and suppliers

Know who owes you money, and who you owe money to at the touch of a button.

Monthly business accounting reports

Wondering whether you are making or losing money? Monthly management accounts allow you to analyse how your business is performing and compare month-by-month or year-by-year.

Access important information and documents quickly

With good bookkeeping you can quickly and easily find information regarding the original sales or expenses in case of disputes or repeat transactions.

Access bank loan, overdraft, or investment information

Keeping good bookkeeping enables you to quickly produce the reports any bank or financial companies require to see before investing in you and your business.

Tax bills and other liabilities

Tax planning is important for everybody, and keeping good records will show you how much tax you are likely to owe allowing you to set some money aside for these bills.

Reduce your accountant's annual fees

You will need an accountant to complete your end-of-year accounts and having good records will reduce your bill, as they will be able to assess your business effectively from the records you have provided.

VAT Returns – filing your tax return

If you are VAT registered you will need to complete a VAT return on a regular basis – monthly, quarterly, or annually. By being organised and using a Making Tax Digital software package will ensure you include everything you are entitled to in any claim or return you make to HMRC.

All of the above will ensure that you can provide your accountant with good records to enable them to prepare your end of year accounts. Here are our recommendations to ensure you are using a good, qualified accountant and bookkeeper.

Good accountants and bookkeepers will help your company grow. Meet and interview several candidates before you decide and be sure to do your background checks.

Here are some suggested research questions to ask yourself when looking to appoint/change accountants:

- Who are they connected to?
- Do they have a strong network of professional people?
- How do they talk about their services?
- Are they enthusiastic and interested in their work?
- Have they received any recommendations from their clients?
- What do those recommendations actually say?

Questions to ask your accountant

- What is their experience?
- How long have they been in business, and what were they doing before?

- What are their qualifications?
- Are they a chartered or certified accountant, a bookkeeper, a financial advisor or something else?
- Are they proactive about saving you money?
- Are they a modern firm with an online accounting software training department?

A good accountant will be able to advise you on what type of business you should be, either self-employed, a partnership or a limited company, and whether you should be VAT registered or not. Remember to always negotiate fees to ensure you are happy that you are receiving good value for money.

You are completing good records and have found the right accountant for your business, so what else do you need to consider to maintain a healthy and successful business?

Get legal advice

We recommend you have your own business terms and conditions. To ensure they will protect you in the event that a dispute arises, we would suggest you ask a solicitor to help you with this.

If you are a partnership, make sure you get partnership agreements drawn up from the beginning. Partnerships start off on a very friendly and informal footing but even the closest of friendships can suffer, so having an agreement in place is invaluable to protect you from anything that may arise in the future.

Business Bbank account

Keeping business and personal finances separate is very important. Ensure you get a business bank account. Keeping all your business income and expenses in your business bank account will enable you to keep clean records for your business from the start.

If you have to put money into the business physically, put that money in the new business bank account, record it as money invested, and once you have enough money in the business to repay that investment, you can pay that money back and record it against the initial investment. This keeps a record of what the business owes you, the investor.

There are a lot of free no-charges bank accounts worth exploring such as Starling, Monzo, and NatWest Online. Most of these banks have saving spaces and create an HMRC Tax Savings Account to keep any potential tax saved for your tax bill at the end of the year.

Get a credit card for cash flow purposes and potential cash back too but pay off the balance every month to avoid interest charges.

Over recent years you will have likely come across the words 'Making Tax Digital' (MTD). What does this actually mean? Making Tax Digital is part of the government's Tax Administration Strategy. It requires businesses and individuals to keep digital records, to use software that works with Making Tax Digital and enables you to submit updates every quarter to HMRC. There has been a staggered introduction to MTD which commenced with larger organisations, followed by any VAT registered companies and is due to be rolled out to all self-employed businesses very soon.

Get MTD (Making Tax Digital) software

Why should I have accounting software?

- It enables you to keep all your bookkeeping records in one place.
- It gives access to your accountant or bookkeeper to make sure you are on track.
- It shows who owes you money.
- It shows who you owe money to.
- It shows if you are making or losing money.
- It shows what you owe in Tax.

What software is out there?

- Xero
- QuickBooks
- Sage
- FreshBooks
- Zoho Books
- FreeAgent

Free or cheap is not always the best. Take a look at Google reviews and talk to modern accountants who understand software. Get a demo and a free trial and set up training to suit your business from the start.

Once you have chosen which software will work best for you and your business you will need to ensure that you set up your software correctly from the start to prevent issues further down the line.

Setting up accounting software

Keep it simple and make it mean something to you and your business.

Create a chart of accounts

It is IMPORTANT to set up your accounts to suit your business and take the time to really understand this section of your accounting software. This will tell you everything financial about your business.

Chart of accounts are individual accounts that you use to record financial transactions. They help you keep track of where money comes from and goes to.

This is the top level of analysing your financial accounts.

The chart of accounts is divided into:

- Revenue accounts – where you record money received by the business.

- Expense accounts – where you record money paid by the business.

- Asset accounts – where you record things that the business owns.

- Liability accounts – where you record debts that the business owes.

- Equity accounts – where you record the funds introduced into the business and drawings by the owner(s).

These can be broken down further and here is a description of terms you may have come across:

- Revenue/income accounts - what type of products and services you provide.

- Direct cost of sales - cost of items or services you provide.

- Expenses/overheads - expenses to run the business including rent, wages, fuel, telephone.

- Assets - what the business owns, customers' outstanding accounts, buildings, stock, money in your bank, equipment.

- Liability accounts - what the business owes, suppliers' outstanding accounts, tax, VAT, wages, loans, credit card balance.

- Equity accounts - Money you have invested or loaned the business.

Accounts Reports

These can be created quickly and easily from your accounting software:

- Profit & Loss – If you have made any money.

- Balance Sheet – What's the business worth?

Your accounting software gives you key data about how your business is performing and which products and services are the most profitable. Here is how you can separate your different products and services:

Products and services

Adding products or services you offer to your accounting software helps you to keep track of what type of products or services are selling and making money. By having your software set up you can easily prepare quotes and invoices in a few clicks for products and services, saving valuable time.

NOTE * If you do have stock, there are lots of additional software applications to help you keep track of stock too.

Customer records

Your accounts can be a great platform to keep up-to-date records of your customers for marketing, quoting, invoicing, recording notes, sending statements and chasing money. You can instantly see what they have purchased, how much they have spent and how regularly they spend with you.

Customer reports instantly tell you:

- Aged receivable - What the customer owes you and what invoices have not been paid.
- Statements – Let the customer know what they owe you.

Supplier records

Keeping an up-to-date record of your suppliers enables you to see what you have bought, how much you have spent, and how regularly you spend with them. It also gives you the data you need should you potentially need to ask for a rebate or discount.

Track all spending. Keep all your bills and receipts by recording them on your accounting software and attach a copy of the bill or receipt to the transaction.

A very easy way to help you match up your payments and receipts is to use additional complementary software that uses an automatic extraction application such as DEXT, Autoentry, or HubDoc. There are many more on the market. This helps streamline this process and save hours in manually entering data.

Supplier reports can be run off to tell you:

- Aged payable - What you owe the supplier and what bills you have not paid.

As well as controlling all your customer and supplier activity you will also need to manage the following:

Bank accounts

Add all your bank accounts, credit cards, and payment methods such as PayPal and Stripe to your accounting software. Record all the transactions that come in and go out of the bank to your accounting software. Paying off customer invoices, paying off supplier bills and recording spent money on receipts.

Keeping a check on your money is important so make sure you record all your income and expenditure too.

One of the most important tasks within your accounting software is to reconcile the bank accounts.

Meaning of reconciliation: Bank reconciliation is a way to double-check your bookkeeping by comparing your business accounts you have recorded in your accounting software against your bank statements. Both sets of records should agree with each other. If not, you need to figure out why.

Once your bank accounts, credit cards, and petty cash accounts have been reconciled, you know you have recorded all your transactions in your accounting software.

Training is available to help set it up to suit your business needs.

VAT Returns

If you are VAT registered it is a legal requirement to submit your VAT return within Making Tax Digital software. If you use your accounting software correctly the software will produce your vat return easily. Make sure you get an expert to help set up your system and get an accountant or good bookkeeper to check your VAT return before submitting.

Payroll

Employing people has a lot of legislation attached and it is important to get HR advice. You will need to pay all employees through a payroll software, there are lots of payroll agencies that take all the stress away from you. If you do decide to do the payroll yourself, please ensure you get help on setting the software up.

If you are looking to grow your business and start employing people, here is the true cost of employing people:

- Agreed gross wage (holiday inc.)
- Company National Insurance
- Pension offering to each employee
- Telephone
- Software
- Computer equipment
- Training
- Insurance
- Clothing
- Working from home allowance
- General overhead – office space, heating, stationery

The true cost of an employee is larger than you think!

We have touched on some of the reports that you can retrieve quickly and easily from your accounting software. Here is a full list:

Business Reports

- Profit & Loss

- Balance Sheet
- Aged Receivables
- Aged Payables
- VAT Return
- Bank Reconciliation Report

Setting up your accounting software can be daunting so ask for help, watch tutorials, get 1-to-1 training, or go on a training course, and make sure your software matches your business. Whilst this may seem to be an extra expense to you and your business, this will be money well spent and will prevent the stress and costs of trying to locate errors further down the line. As business owners, we love what we do and we do it to earn a living but we are often not very good at chasing our money. It is so important to have a professional approach to money. This is not a hobby; they have had your services and products and owe you that money. Client relations will be affected when money is outstanding. Chase it up in a timely manner to avoid future conflict.

Credit control

Cash flow is so important for the day-to-day running of your business, and I refer to the saying *'turnover is vanity, profit is sanity and cash is king'*.

Turnover is Vanity - turnover is important in your business but it is 'vanity' unless your business is profitable.

Profit is Sanity - this speaks for itself. We need to make a profit to remain in business.

Cash is King – this in the amount of liquid money you have in your business.

What is credit control?

This is purely a business process that promotes the selling of goods or services by extending credit to customers, which can be 7, 14, or 30 days, but you are still giving them a time of credit before they pay. I suppose in effect this is an interest-free loan.

To determine how much you are willing to loan them/offer a credit period. There are a number of checks I believe you should follow. You may wish to carry out a credit check if the work you are doing for the client is of high monetary value. There are a number of companies that can offer this service such as Experian, Credit Check, and Credit Safe to name a few.

Make sure you state in writing your payment terms and conditions on your invoices, something like '*Payment is due 30 days from invoice date*'. If needed, you may require a contract with your client. For this you may need to gain approval via your solicitor.

A benefit is to offer them multiple ways to pay such as bank details for a BACS payment, a 'Pay Now' button, or ways to sign-up to a direct debit facility, or Crezco.

When you have agreed to start business with a customer create a template to get as much information as you can about them.

Include the following:

- Customer name
- Full company billing address
- Telephone number, email address
- Delivery address
- Name of director(s)
- Company registration number
- VAT number
- Sales contact
- Purchase order if required
- Two references (ask your peers if they have dealt with this company before)
- Date and signature

Send regular monthly statements of account - this is a step for your customer to check they have the invoices stated. There are a number of companies that will only pay once they have a statement and can check these off and figures agree.

So, you have raised your invoice, and this has been sent out to your new customer. What next?

- Place a courtesy call to the payer, it may be the director, or the sales team who need to approve this and pass it to accounts. Understand their process. If it's the finance team, check you are emailing the correct person. How often is their payment run, monthly or weekly? Is everything correct on the invoice including a description of work carried out? A five-minute call in my experience can cover a number of unnecessary emails and people really do appreciate this personal touch.
- If the payment date has passed, send a statement for a nudge to remind them and make another friendly call.
- Your next step would be to send an overdue letter, followed by a final demand. Keep notes of these with dates as this is evidence that you have attempted to recover the amount owing using the correct steps.
- If these are ignored you can proceed to start the legal process with a Letter Before Action (LBA) and then if needed, start the legal action. There are a number of debt collection agencies who can assist at this stage so there is always someone who can give you clear advice.

DID YOU KNOW you can charge a daily statutory interest rate on invoices that have exceeded their due date? This is 8% plus the Bank of England base rate for all business-to-business transactions.

With my years of experience in credit control, I know there can be an awkward time where you have worked alongside your customer, produced great work or supplied a service, and payment has not been made as agreed. How do you approach this? This is where you need someone in your team or even an outsourced team who does not have a personal attachment and sees it as a business transaction that requires payment. It takes away that difficult call or email and you can always say you have a robust credit control process.

Case Study

I worked with a client who had completed some work for his 'mate', who I was requested not to contact as he would pay, no problem. Six months later the invoice was still unpaid, and I was allowed to step in. Unfortunately, this case did go to court and the customer had to pay all the costs that had accrued. Let someone else deal with your credit control, as it also shows you have a professional approach to money in your business.

Schedule regular time to check your money that's owed to you after you have checked and reconciled. Ensuring your business financial records are up to date and regularly monitored is essential for all businesses. Keeping on top of money in and money out gives you an accurate overview of your business enabling you to make important financial decisions. By keeping up to date records your accountant or business advisor will be able to advise you regarding tax and other financial decisions. Set time aside each month to analyse your business finances to ensure you are making money.

14: Networking

By Sharon Louca

Is Business Networking part of your marketing and growth plan? Starting your own business is an exciting journey filled with new possibilities and opportunities. Already in this book we have covered many of the key areas you need to consider right from the conception of your idea, the planning and financial stages, through to the logistics and marketing of your business. Whether you're following a dream or passion, creating a better work-life balance, or something else, there's so much to look forward to when you are your own boss.

However, it's important to remember that running a business is not without its challenges. There's a steep learning curve, and you'll need to develop resilience, tenacity, and perseverance to be successful. You don't need a university degree or a long list of qualifications to be a successful business owner, but you do need to have the inner strength and determination to make it work.

Since 2009, at the very beginning of my business journey, I have been actively engaged in business networking. I cannot stress enough how profoundly networking has shaped the progress and direction of my business. The incredible people I have met, the invaluable mentors and friends I have made, and the amazing opportunities that have come my way – all have played a key role in my business success story.

In this chapter I will share with you my own experiences along with the advantages and a few disadvantages of business networking. As an award-winning networker and multiple business owner, I can confidently affirm that business networking has been an absolute game-changer for me. And I can assure you, I am not alone in this sentiment; many of my co-contributing authors to this book will wholeheartedly echo this sentiment.

As a shy introvert immersing myself into the business networking community was very much outside of my comfort zone. Mixing with strangers where I had to stand up and talk about myself while all eyes were on me, made me feel like bolting for the door never to return. If this is the reaction you have when anyone mentions business networking, you are not alone, and I totally understand how you feel. However, let me assure you that feeling will be short-lived. Networking events are not the scary meetings you think they are and when you find the right place for you, the feelings you will experience are completely the opposite – a sense of belonging, a safe space, a community feel. Networking is an excellent way for small businesses to raise awareness of their products and services and get to meet the people behind the business. One of the most important things you can do when starting your own business is to find a supportive network of like-minded women. Being an entrepreneur can be a lonely journey, and it's essential to have people around you who have been there before and can offer guidance and support.

Networking has had a bad reputation over the years and been known as the 'old boys' network, a very male-orientated world of power suits and pressure to make referrals. I am pleased to report that since 2013 there have been so many independent networking groups formed, and the online space has exploded since 2020, and there really is now something out there to suit everyone.

There are groups that focus on the different elements of networking:-
- Connecting people
- Passing business leads and referrals
- Gaining help and support
- Increasing business knowledge
- Personal development
- Collaboration opportunities

At Women's Business Network we are proud to say we have combined all these elements into our networking offering. Other groups may focus on purely one or two elements. Whether you prefer to network from your pc or venture out and meet people face to face, you can find a group to suit your needs.

Here are some of the many benefits of business networking.

Access to a supportive community:

One of the biggest benefits of networking is being able to connect with other like-minded women who are facing similar challenges and opportunities as you. Experiences and knowledge shared makes you realise you are not alone in how you are feeling and there are always options out there for you. You can connect with other like-minded professional women to gain the help, advice and support you deserve.

Increase your visibility and brand awareness

When starting out in business it can be hard to get the message out about yourself and your business. It is difficult to stand out and gain traction amongst all the noise of social media and unless you are willing to invest in optimising your website it is likely you will be invisible to your ideal clients. Whereas in an environment where you are mixing with business-people, who are getting to know you and your business, you are creating visibility for yourself and your products/services. Women are excellent at forming relationships and networking is the ideal platform for these relationships to be developed and nurtured.

Access to new business opportunities

When like-minded women come together it is amazing some of the ideas and brainstorming that takes place. Collaboration opportunities arise when businesses with products and services that complement each other come together. For example; hairdressers and makeup artists, wedding venues and florists, accountants and bookkeepers, solicitors and accountants, and the list goes on. The services they offer complement one another. Often one client will require both services, and if you are offering a package which combines the two, that can be of great advantage to your ideal clients and help you to stand out from your competition. Being able to offer your client more than one service all under the one roof works well for both parties, you and the client. It also opens new avenues and revenue streams for your business. Many business partnerships and membership groups have been formed because of collaboration opportunities.

Enhance your business knowledge

When you start out in business you cannot possibly know all there is to know about running a business. Networking is a perfect platform for you to develop your business and personal development knowledge at low cost. Many groups have guest speakers who will share their area of expertise and give you handy hints and tips for you to implement in your business. There are often lots of free and paid workshops on all areas of running a business that you get to hear about in the networking arena. You will hear about new changes coming, and whether technological or legal, you can pick up a huge array of information and business knowledge from people you meet through networking, information you would not necessarily get to hear about elsewhere, especially when you are so busy running your own business. It helps you to ensure your business remains compliant and lawful.

Mentorship and guidance

The mentors I met in my early days in business had a huge impact on me and my business. They were people who were willing to spare their time free of charge to share with me the lessons they had learned so that I wouldn't make the same mistakes they had made. They challenged my ideas or ways of thinking, not to deter me from my plans but to enable me to gain focus and clarity and ensure that I was following the right path for me. Those mentors are the reason I chose to pay it forward and start supporting others through my own networking groups.

Increased self-confidence

I am shy and introvert by nature, I have always had inner self-confidence in my ability but that didn't always come across due to my shyness. Spending time with people who want the best for you, who share your highs and lows and a place where you feel safe and supported all help to increase your confidence. In a place where you feel supported you can step outside your comfort zone and stretch yourself without the fear of rejection. Encouragement and feedback from your fellow peers are extremely useful too.

Resources

Many networking groups can provide you with resources i.e., templates or guides that you can use in your business. They may be able to provide you with information about where you can access funding, some groups like ours have expert panels where you can gain free advice on key areas of your business.

Personal and professional growth

Whilst growing my businesses I have also worked on my own personal development. I have learnt so much about myself and gained a better understanding of what makes me who I am and I have learnt to embrace my uniqueness. When we work alone, we are more likely to stay inside our comfort zone, however, when we hear others' success stories it is an incentive to push ourselves and want more.

Opportunities for collaboration

This book is the result of a collaboration of like-minded businesswomen. Other collaborations may be hosting workshops or events. When women come together to discuss issues that are affecting us all, collectively we have a voice and can make a bigger impact on the world than one person alone. This leads to positive change and empowerment of other women and for the generations to follow.

Alternative ways of thinking and working

Networking exposes women to diverse ranges of perspectives and ideas. This leads to more creative thinking and innovation which is so important. Mixing with like-minded women can create new ways of working which can have a huge impact on both your business and your income.

Increased business and referrals

The sole reason most of us go networking in the beginning is to gain clients and increase our revenue. Networking works when you take the time to build strong, trusted relationships. People buy from people who they know, like and trust. That is why people who don't make sales in the first couple of meetings determine that networking doesn't work. Think about how you buy. Do you hate hard-sell tactics or people not taking time to get to know you and just wanting a sale? When you take time to build that know, like and trust, then the referrals will follow and it's not necessarily from the people in the room. It is about who they know and who they can introduce you to.

Are there any disadvantages to business networking?

You need to be consistent with networking. Don't assume you can show up to 2 or 3 meetings and the work will start rolling in. Networking does come at a cost to both your pocket and your time, therefore ensure you are getting a return for your investment on networking. I cover this topic in chapter 16. Here are a few more things to remember.

Meeting new people

When meeting new people for the first time it is very easy to get drawn in and believe everything someone tells you. My recommendation would be to always follow your gut instinct about the person you are talking to. Go away and verify information they have given you. With the power of social media and the internet it is very easy to 'check people out'.

Don't feel pressured to join a group immediately

With so much choice in networking events, do not feel pressured to join on the first visit. Any reputable group will encourage you to visit them more than once to ensure the group is the right fit for you.

Networking means not working

A solopreneur has many roles in the business, so your time is likely to be in short supply. Attending events especially when face to face can take you away from your business for many hours. Ensure that the events you are attending are worthwhile to you and your business. Having a plan and strategy before attending means this time is less likely to be wasted. I cover this more in chapter 16.

As you can see there are far more advantages than disadvantages to business networking and when you have a clear strategy in place you can ensure you get a return on your time and money investment.

As I alluded to earlier, I am a multi-award-winning networker. Who would have thought that shy woman who stood shaking in her stilettos at her first meeting would go on to be centre stage accepting two networking awards in 2022? It has not always been an easy ride. I have had to work hard to overcome my fears and nerves, but I wouldn't change a thing. It's all part of my personal and business growth story. Whether you are an introvert or extrovert you can make business networking work for you. I hope from this chapter you can now see that networking provides far more than just a place to meet like-minded people. Will you now be making business networking part of your marketing strategy for your business?

Whether you are new to networking or a seasoned professional I truly hope you are getting everything you need from the groups you attend and if not, then please do your research and find new groups that will meet those needs. I would love to welcome you to a Women's Business Network meeting one day soon.

Part 2

Surviving and Thriving

15: The Importance of Getting Regular Enquiries

By Colette Bratton

If you're a small business owner, you need to keep your business visible. Otherwise, how will prospects be able to enquire or buy from you?

However, some entrepreneurs find promoting their small businesses quite overwhelming. They can struggle with knowing where to start, as well as how to find the time to work on marketing their company. As a result, small business marketing can be undertaken quite sporadically, as entrepreneurs struggle to find the time and the focus, even though they realise how important marketing is to grow their businesses. That's why some entrepreneurs end up on the small business roller coaster, where the number of leads generated varies dramatically from month to month. One month there may be a decent volume of enquiries, then the month after, a downturn. A deluge of leads one month, then a drought the next, so if the results were graphed, they might look similar to the latest thrill ride at a theme park with all the ups and downs! And it's often just down to inconsistent marketing activity.

It's easily done. When a business owner has lots of work in, there isn't much time to work on marketing the business. Then, when that work is completed and the business isn't so busy, the marketing activity begins again. This stop-and-start marketing activity isn't conducive to generating regular enquiries and prevents a business from getting any kind of marketing momentum! Being on the small business roller coaster is hard work. It's what can stop you taking your business to the next level and hold you back from growing your business to where you want it to be. The good news is, it is possible to stop the huge ups and downs and create a more stable level of enquiries into your business each month, just by being more consistent with your marketing efforts.

Whilst there are too many external influences for the number of enquiries coming into your business to stay exactly the same each month, the right marketing activity done consistently can help you change the peaks and troughs into more gentle curves and waves. Create a strategy to help you get a more consistent number of enquiries into your business.

Here are some tips to get started.

Analyse your current situation

Take some time to think about your business. Make a list of what's working well, and what's not working well, especially in terms of leads, enquiries, and sales. Have a think about where most of your leads come from. Also think about your workload throughout the years, to calculate any busy and quiet times. Are there certain times of the year that your business is quieter than others? If you're aware of these times, you can implement some marketing activity in the run-up, to try to increase your sales opportunities during this period.

Give your business a marketing review.

Do an honest review of your current marketing activity.

- How well do you know your target audience? If you've not got a clear idea of who your customers are, it will make it harder for you to target them effectively.

- What marketing collateral do you currently have (website, leaflets, business cards, social media accounts etc.)? Does the information on any of these need updating? Is there anything new you need to create?

- What kind of customer and prospect database do you have? Do you have all your customer and prospect details in a safe, easy-to-access customer relationship management (CRM) system that allows you to communicate to your prospects and customers regularly? Or are these details buried in accounts systems or paper files and therefore difficult to utilise?

- How active are you with your marketing? How often do you create new marketing content and collateral, post on social media, update your website information, write a new blog or send out direct mail or emails? How could you improve the visibility of your business even further?

- How well does your business appear on search engines? If you perform a search that your target audience might undertake if they were looking for a supplier of your type of products and services, where does your business appear in the search rankings?

Whilst you're reviewing the search results, take a note of which other companies that are similar to yours come up when you search for a term that your ideal client might type in, so you can review your competition. This will help you work out your unique selling point (USP), to help identify what makes your business different. What's the reason someone may choose to buy from you rather than your competition? Once you identify your USP, you can use it in your marketing content, to help promote the advantages of using your business and help prospects with their buying decisions.

Once you've had a good look at your business by doing the above review tasks, create a plan to help you become more consistent with your marketing.

Here are some tips to help you generate more regular leads:

- Think about your customer journey. How can you spread the word about your business to your ideal prospects? For example, there are a number of ways you can help people find out more about your products and services, including social media, email marketing, networking, direct mail, advertising, and guest speaking opportunities.

- Then think about your sales funnel. Once you've had interest from a prospect, how do you take that prospect to the next stage of the buying journey.

- Make sure to always include a call to action in your marketing communications, such as a link to your website, subscription offer or free trial/demo.

- Think about using lead magnets as part of your marketing efforts, such as free trainings, e-books, downloads and/or webinars that prospects can sign-up for (helping you grow your email database at the same time!).

- Check your website is working hard enough for your business. Many people use search engines like Google when looking for product or service suppliers. So, do what you can to make sure your website is working as hard as it needs to, so it gets your business found in the right searches to help you generate more enquiries.

- Keep your website content fresh by adding regular news stories and blogs. Not only can this help your website in searches, but writing regular blogs is a great way to showcase your expertise and talk about issues that will help your target audience find and identify with you.

- Another way for local businesses to get found online is to use Google's free Business Profile tool (also known as Google My Business), that offers more details about your company when your business is searched, to help you stand out from the competition. You can add photos, events, posts, offers, and there's even a question-and-answer section to help prospects understand more about your business offering.

- Don't forget to collect reviews and testimonials. Social proof is very powerful, so remember to collect reviews and testimonials about your business. Google reviews are definitely worth collecting, as they can help with searches – but don't limit reviews only to Google! You can ask for testimonials in many other ways too. Your clients can leave reviews on social media platforms like Facebook and LinkedIn or email you their feedback directly. And don't forget to include testimonials on your company website and in other marketing collateral such as leaflets and brochures. Customer testimonials can also make great social media posts too – just use a design app to turn their comments into pretty posts!

- Use your CRM (customer relationship management) system. If you've got (or can develop) a database of your prospects and your customers (past and present) then you'll have a fantastic asset that you can use to help promote your business. Whether that's for telemarketing, email marketing or direct mail, think about keeping in touch with these people who have at some stage made contact with your company, in order to keep your business at the forefront of their minds. Just be careful to comply with all the relevant data protection and data usage laws!

- Remember that sales opportunities don't just come from new prospects. Additional orders can come from existing customers too, so make sure you keep your existing (and previous) customers up to date with what you're offering, by keeping in touch with them regularly so they are aware of the whole range of products and services your business offers – not just the ones they have already used you for!

- Networking is a great way to promote your business, and these days it can be done in-person or online, allowing people to network in all kinds of places, not just their local area! Find a group that you like and start to build some good contacts and relationships.

- Look for collaboration opportunities with other businesses. If you can create relationships with businesses that have a similar target audience to you, but offer different products or services, then these relationships can sometimes be quite fruitful. The wedding industry is a great example of how collaboration can work well. Cake makers, bridal shops, wedding car services, venues, celebrants, etc. can all work together to recommend each other to engaged couples, for everyone's benefit (including the happy couple who are often delighted to be informed about other great suppliers!). Get your thinking cap on about who you could collaborate with in your industry.

- Showcase your successes by creating case studies about the work you do, to help prospects understand how you help people. You might even consider issuing a press release to the media about your business if you have a newsworthy story!

There are many other ways you can promote your business, including shows, exhibitions, directories, door drops, podcasts, etc.

Remember, the only way to get more customers is to shout about your business. And the best way to do that is with some kind of marketing! Whatever you struggle with when it comes to marketing your business, whether it's knowing what to do, how to do it, when to do it, how to find time to do it, or having the confidence to do it, then find a way.

Find a way to get the knowledge, motivation, support, and accountability you need to do a little bit of marketing on your business regularly.

16: How to Achieve a Return on Investment in Business Networking

By Sharon Louca

Business networking forms part of most female entrepreneurs' marketing plans and is just one of the many ways we choose to market our businesses. We talked about networking and its advantages and disadvantages earlier in chapter 11.

Networking is important because it holds the power of two-way human connection where you can build trust and create strong connections with like-minded people who can help you and your business. This is much harder to achieve purely via your website, social media content or other marketing channels. To recap, networking is not just a place to sell your wares, it is where you will meet mentors and friends. You will increase your business knowledge through the people you meet and the speakers you listen to.

Running a business as a female entrepreneur can be very lonely. Finding like-minded people who understand you and have been where you are now, and who can share with you words of wisdom, can make a huge difference. Too many women give up on their dreams of running a business because it all becomes too hard, and they have no one to turn to. That was one of the driving forces behind my decision to launch my own networking support groups in 2014.

Networking is an excellent marketing tool but as with any activity in your business it should be measured for its success and to ensure you are receiving a return on investment. What does this mean? There is a cost element to networking both financially for subscriptions and meeting costs plus your time, so you need to ensure you are gaining something back in terms of connections, sales, knowledge, support etc.

Networking works if you work at it. The clue 'work' is in the word itself. "You get out what you put in." Networking is not a quick win but done well can reap huge rewards for you and your business. In this chapter we will look at how to set goals for your networking activities, ensuring you are attending the right events for you, the importance of creating meaningful relationships, and what to do before, during and after the event to create revenue and results. And finally, how you can measure your activities to find out the true cost/revenue.

Networking goals

What do you want to achieve from your networking activities? Not having a goal/plan when attending networking events may result in you feeling you have just wasted valuable time that could have been better spent. Setting goals gives you a focus on why you are attending the meeting. Common goals can revolve around building a support network, raising brand awareness, finding new business opportunities, building your knowledge, making new connections. To really ensure that you meet those goals make them SMART - Specific, Measurable, Achievable, Relevant and Time Bound. Here is an example: Let's make building a support network a SMART goal:

Specific: I want to meet people that will help me to build my confidence, a place where I can ask for help for me and my business. I am looking to meet fellow women in business who have more experience than me. Questions I need to ask myself:

- Am I looking to get this from one group or my chosen individuals?
- What type of group do I need – mixed or women only?
- How many people and what experience do they need to have had?
- What values do they need to have to be compatible with me?

By drilling down to specifics, we can then make the goal measurable:

Measurable: You determine you want help with marketing, finance and sales. Ask yourself:

- I am looking to find 3 mentors with this area of expertise.
- Are people with these areas of expertise available in one group?

Achievable: Based on the meetings you have been attending ask yourself:

- Am I meeting the right people who can help me?
- Can I find other groups that may be a better fit for me?
- Do I know where to look, i.e., networking groups, social media?

Relevant: Ask yourself:

- Is this goal relevant for me to set right now?
- Do I have the time to consistently show up so I can achieve this goal?

- Is this goal important to me?

Timebound: Ask yourself:

- What timescale am I going to set myself to join a new group or get these mentors on board?
- Decide on the timescale and keep to working on it.

Think about what you want to get out of networking and what steps you need to put into place to make it happen, break it down and make it SMART.

Let's give you another example.

Specific: This goal is specific:

I am new to networking, and I have no connections. I want to build my connections and database to 50 new connections per month.

Measurable: This goal is measurable:

I want to make 50 new connections this month.

Achievable: This goal is achievable:

I am booked on 10 events this month. To meet my target, I need to make at least 5 connections at each meeting.

How will I do this? I will collect contact details from all attendees via online chat or business cards, etc.

Relevant: This goal is relevant:

I am new to business and to grow, I need to build my connections for a variety of reasons. To gain support, raise my brand awareness and to gain referrals. This is important to me.

Timebound: This goal is timebound:

By the end of the month, I am confident I will have 50 new contacts.

Can you see how setting yourself these goals gives you a focus rather than just turning up at a networking event, having a nice chat with people and going away without taking any action?

What target can you set for yourself for your networking activities?

Targeted Networking

To get the most out of networking and to ensure you meet your networking goals you want to identify networking groups or events that are best suited to you, your business and where your ideal clients are going to be. Online events are a great way to meet lots of people and attend lots of events because you can work up until a few minutes before the meeting and be back working again when the meeting ends. Face-to-face events must factor in travelling time, so do your research to make sure the event is suitable, establish that people you want to connect with will be there, and who the event is targeted at. Do this before committing so you are not wasting valuable time.

How can you determine which events to attend?

Attend events targeted for your business sector and if you prefer women-only events, opt for those. Meetings have a variety of formats – relaxed, informal networking, where you will need to work the room, structured meetings where everyone gets to speak and introduce themselves, business expo's where you can mix with attendees and exhibitors. Weigh up the pros and cons for each event based on your availability and meeting your networking goals. If you know that you gain more success from structured networking meetings, opt for them over informal networking. Where is your time best spent? As a female entrepreneur running her own business, the biggest impact of all of this is our time. Use it well by researching events for suitability, and if possible, find out expected attendee numbers or who is likely to be there.

Think about your business and whether it is location-specific as this will determine which groups you choose to attend. Online meetings often attract a national audience which as a customer-facing business may not be appropriate. For example, a dog-groomer, hairdresser or electrician will have a distinct geographical area.

Creating meaningful relationships

As women we are very good at forging strong relationships. We are good listeners, we care about each other, and genuinely want each other to succeed. We are nurturers by nature so when we take the time to engage and support, we receive it back in return. Building relationships is at the heart of being a successful networker. Another trait of a successful networker is to be a good listener. Taking a genuine interest in others and their businesses creates an excellent impression to others of the kind of person you are, and they will want to help you in return. You become memorable so when a contact is asked if they know someone who does what you do, they will talk about you to them. The more focused you are on selecting your networking groups and events the more you will gain. Our group WBN, is solely focused on supporting women running their own businesses and providing them with a safe, trusted support network where they can gain advice and support, increase business knowledge, and grow in confidence. We are very clear on what we offer and who we help so our visitors know what they can expect.

Building strong relationships increases business sales but also many other opportunities. Some of the opportunities I have been given as a result of networking are a 50% share in a client's business, I became a published author of two books via networking, I have entered numerous awards events and have won three, I have been interviewed on various podcasts, been interviewed for radio and TV, and I have been a judge and sponsor at awards events. I was invited to become a committee member for a brain tumour charity, which is very close to my heart, called The Giles Trust during a networking meeting.

The forging of strong relationships also provides women with people to turn to in times of need, when you are having a bad day and imposter syndrome has kicked in. Just a conversation with a trusted connection can completely turn around your day and quickly get you back on track. Without that kind of support the future can often look very bleak indeed.

Measuring ROI

How can you measure your return on investment for your networking activities? By measuring your activities and results.

Before you do that, here are some hints and tips on what you can do before, during and after each event to increase your chances of a good return on investment:

Before:

- Choose your events carefully.

- Commit to regularly attending groups you join.

- Ask for a speaker slot to further demonstrate your expertise.

- Are you representing yourself and your brand effectively - think about your outfit, your business cards, and promotional items.

- Prepare what you are going to say so you come across with a clear message and everyone understands what you do. Be memorable and demonstrate your area of expertise.

During the meeting:

- Don't just head for people you know – speak to new people.

- Sit next to different people, this is more difficult in online groups, but the hosts tend to try and mix up the rooms, so you get to chat with different people.

- Share your business cards/contact details.

After the meeting:

- Connect with people via email and social media channels.

- Arrange to have a follow up call or meet them for a coffee to start to get to know more about each other.

- Can you add the contact to your mailing list – please observe their rights under data protection and ask their permission - do not spam them.

- Record who you met at what meetings via your CRM (customer relationship management system) or other method, i.e., spreadsheet, so you can continue to develop your relationship and stay in touch.

So, we have looked at how we can set goals, how we select the events we attend, what to do before, during and after the meeting. Now let's look at how we can measure the results of all these activities.

A simple calculation you can do:

Work out how much you have spent at networking over a set period, i.e., per month, per quarter or per year. **Tip**: set up a nominal code in your accounting software for networking and then you can easily see your expenditure. Now work out the value of sales that have been achieved because of your networking efforts, based on referrals from networking. Again, you may be able to tag these sales in your accounting software to make this another easy calculation. Deduct the cost of networking from the Sales Achieved to see whether it is a + or - figure. This will tell you the true cost or value of your networking activities.

However, when analysing this information don't forget to factor in what else you have received, i.e., opportunities, gained knowledge, met mentors who have helped you, and if you are more confident now because of your networking efforts. Whilst these may not carry a monetary value, what they have given you is of much more value to you and the future of your business. Your confidence and your knowledge that could prevent you from making costly mistakes, the ability to keep up with latest technology and trends, can all be learned via networking without any additional direct cost. Here you have invested in your personal and business development at no additional costs to your business. Add to that the personal brand awareness that can be achieved through public speaking, entering awards, sponsoring events. The opportunities for collaboration - this book is the result of collaboration between our WBN members. We often see our members who have complementing services work on projects together where they can share their products/services with their combined contact lists/databases, again creating more opportunities and revenue.

In conclusion, if you have not ventured into the world of business networking, I hope this chapter has revealed to you that there is so much more on offer than just pitching up and selling your wares. When you have a clear plan or goal to work with you are much more likely to succeed. As the quote by Benjamin Franklin says,

"If you fail to plan, you are planning to fail."

By taking time to prepare before the meeting you are going to make a bigger impact, be recognised, and remembered for your expertise. By committing and attending regularly you will nurture strong relationships and create the supportive network every woman deserves when running her own business. By measuring your successes through networking, you will clearly see where you are reaping the rewards and to where your attention should be dedicated, not forgetting that all rewards don't necessarily have a £ in front of them.

Now it's over to you to implement a networking strategy into your business networking activities. Good luck on your networking journey and I would love to meet you one day at one of our WBN meetings.

17: Make Marketing Your Business Manageable

By Colette Bratton

Some entrepreneurs find themselves overwhelmed when they think about marketing. Being a business owner can be hard enough without the many marketing tasks you're supposed to try to squeeze in regularly. There are so many marketing activities, online and offline to choose from that it's sometimes difficult to know where to start. Even posting on social media has become more complicated. It used to involve posting on your main feed, but now there are stories and reels to think about too!

Here are seven tips to help make your marketing activity more manageable.

1. Identify your ideal customer

Identifying your ideal customer and understanding your target audience will help you manage the marketing of your business. Questions like, "Where should I market my business?" and "What content should I write?" can be answered easily once research has been done on the target audience. Understanding your ideal client helps you to save time and money on your marketing activities as you don't waste valuable time creating content that doesn't resonate. You also save money by only promoting your business in places that your ideal customer is likely to be. If you haven't spent time doing some work on your ideal client, it's worth putting some time aside.

2. Create great content

Ramping up the quality of your content on social media, blogs, and news stories so it resonates with your ideal customers can help to improve results and make your marketing easier. What are your ideal customers interested in reading about? You'll find a few suggestions below.

- What might they want to know about your products and services? What questions might they have about your business that you can answer in your content?

- What could you share about your business that they'd find interesting – about your team, your plans, your customers, or some behind the scenes sneak peeks?

- What are you doing today / this week / this month that you could share as news? Any exciting places you're visiting for business? What interesting projects are you working on?

- What's happening around the world that's relevant to your business? News, awareness days, etc.

- What can you tell them about you, the business owner, to help them know, like and trust you? Perhaps some information about how you ended up running your business, snippets about your business life, and maybe some insight into your future plans could create some interesting content.

Content is king, so take time to research your audience and plan some great content. Don't forget you can repurpose and recycle content too, to help you make your content schedule even more manageable.

3. Harness the benefits of batching

Marketing is so much harder if you're doing it from scratch, so plan and batch instead. Batching is the art of grouping similar jobs, so you do them together instead of flitting between tasks and getting distracted. There are lots of marketing activities where you can use this strategy. You can batch your general content creation, by putting some time aside to brainstorm ideas. That way you can create your own logbook of content ideas to work from, that you can turn into blogs, social media, news articles, PR stories, or whatever you want.

You can easily batch your social media, including thinking of content ideas, finding and selecting images/videos and even scheduling/posting. Decide what period of time you'd like to batch the content for and work on it. Then you've got everything you need for this week, or this month's social media. All sorted! And you can easily amend the schedule if anything unexpectedly exciting turns up.

You can batch your blog post ideas. If you are committed to producing a monthly blog post, you can plan and batch the titles for your blog posts for the next 3,6 or even 12 months. You don't have to write all the blogs at this stage but write some notes with ideas about what you could write about each month, maybe with some work-in-progress titles. That way, you can make sure the topics work in sequence, and just finish writing the blog posts before you need them.

You can follow the same planning and batching process for your regular newsletter. Just plan out some notes about what you want to include in the next edition, or even the next two or three editions.

You could also batch your 60-second scripts if you do regular networking, and perhaps even tie these in with your social media or blog/news content. Not only does planning and batching save you time, but it also helps you be more consistent. We all know that if a task feels like hard work, it's harder to get started. There's nothing harder than staring at a blank piece of paper or screen when you don't know what to write. Once you've batched some ideas, that's the hardest bit started and it's relatively easy to finish the rest. If you don't enjoy writing copy, you could consider outsourcing this task by passing your ideas over to a copywriter or virtual assistant for them to turn into finished marketing material for you. Read the chapter about outsourcing later in this book for more help with this.

4.   Dedicate time to work ON your business.

Successful business owners dedicate time to work 'on' rather than just 'in' their businesses. Put time aside to work on the strategic aspects of your business, such as marketing. Don't keep saying you need to find the time - put some time in your diary. As busy business owners, there are never enough hours in a day. If you try to squeeze your marketing into the gaps then it won't happen, because there are no gaps! Work tasks can easily expand to fill the time we have available. Schedule marketing time in your diary regularly and use it to do whatever needs to be done. Plan your strategy, create your content, work on new lead generation ideas and make those follow-up calls. If you find you're too distracted in your usual place of work, perhaps look for somewhere else to get strategic and creative. Take your notebook and/or laptop to a quiet coffee shop or library, and work on your marketing there. Ringfence your marketing time and prioritise it. Try your hardest not to cancel or re-schedule it. Marketing your business is a priority because it's what brings in future clients and customers.

5.   Work to a plan!

It's hard to market your business if you don't have a plan. Take some time to create a plan, so you know:

- what marketing channels you're going to use.

- what content you're going to issue.

- how often you're going to undertake your marketing activity, how many times each week/month are you going to post on social media, send out a newsletter, write a blog, add some news to your website etc.

- what marketing steps need to be put in place to help a prospect move down the sales funnel to become a customer.

- how you're going to monitor your results.

Taking the time to plan it out will help you put it all in place, as you can tackle it in manageable chunks.

6. Utilise tools to make your marketing easier

We're very fortunate in this day and age that there are a number of tools that can help us make marketing our businesses easier. Here are a few that may be useful:

- E-newsletter tools, that you can use to send out online newsletters to your prospects and customers, to keep them up to date with what's happening in your business.

- Scheduling tools, to help you schedule your content in advance.

- Design tools, to help you create flyers, e-books and interesting social media graphics.

- Survey tools, to help you send questionnaires out to your audience to find out more about them and capture their thoughts about your business.

- Customer Relationship Management (CRM) systems, to help you keep track of all your prospects and customers.

- Analytics tools, to help you track important statistics such as website traffic and social media activity.

- Project management tools, that can be extremely helpful whether you're working alone or as part of a wider team.

- Marketing Diary/Planner, because it's useful to have somewhere to log all your strategy and ideas, plus important information about your ideal customer, keywords, hashtags, content ideas, appointments, marketing and lead generation activity.

- Notebook/Notes app for new ideas, to log interesting content ideas or growth plans, as every entrepreneur needs somewhere to note down their good ideas for future reference.

7. Do, delegate or delay!

Make a plan about what needs to be done, then decide what you need to 'do, delegate or delay'. Being a small business owner doesn't mean you have to do everything. In fact, it's pretty impossible for you to do everything when there are only 24 hours in each day! Not everything needs to be done now. Some tasks can be parked for later. It's important to prioritise. Work out what needs to be done, decide when it needs to be done and specify who needs to do it. Look at the most urgent tasks to decide which only you can do, and which ones could be outsourced. Use your valuable time productively, so that the time you are spending on marketing can start to bring you better results.

Try implementing some of the seven steps above to help you move from overwhelmed to organised when it comes to marketing your small business.

18: The Power of Storytelling

By Shelley Wilson

Starting a business is a big deal, but as you navigate the journey of entrepreneurship you may begin to lose a sense of why you started, or even why you are continuing on this path.

I began my first business (a holistic health spa) in 2008, just as a recession hit the UK. As a single parent of three young children, I tried to hide my sheer panic behind buoyant marketing and special offers. However, that business is not the same one I am running today. The recession was hard, but I survived and even thrived. It was an illness that eventually thwarted my plans for world domination.

Fast forward fifteen years, and I find myself writing for a living, which is something the younger me dreamt about but never believed possible. My holistic business was wonderful, and I came away from that experience with lots of happy memories, friends, and lessons. Life stuff steered me down a different route and I had to turn my hobby of writing into a main source of income pretty much overnight.

As it happens, I adore being able to write for a living. Storytelling is something I find fascinating and powerful. Helping my clients, colleagues, and audience understand the benefits of stories outside of the confines of a paperback is something I'm passionate about. As I mentioned, starting a business is a big deal and you will, no doubt, have a valid reason for doing so. For me, it was the freedom to spend more time with my children and also to help women feel better about themselves. As a survivor of domestic abuse, having a platform that enabled me to empower women spurred me on – and still does.

What's your why? Why did you start your business?

I see so many business owners churning out the same marketing ploys online, trying to fit into a hole (or trend) that strips their authenticity. They miss out on valuable opportunities because they have detached from their stories. There is only one you, and your unique experiences shape your life and business choices. These are your stories, and they are an incredibly powerful tool for any business owner.

How a post about breakfast boosted my business visibility

When I talk about the power of storytelling for business owners I'm often met with a confused expression and a lot of questions.

- What stories should I tell?
- Who on earth would be interested in me?
- But my life/business is so dull!

When I dig a little deeper, I usually discover a treasure trove of adventures, interests, and skills that aren't always obvious from a client's small LinkedIn headline. Using a few open questions helps people remember old hobbies, and long-forgotten experiences, and always unearths a humorous tale or two! Using storytelling in your business marketing doesn't need a trip down memory lane. In fact, your day-to-day meetings, networking, and life is a gold mine of content and stories. Take for instance my post about breakfast which I shared on LinkedIn. It proved to be one of my most popular posts amassing over 13,000 impressions, a flurry of new followers, and lots of chatter and engagement in the comment feed.

The post read as follows:

My favourite time of the week is Friday Breakfast.
"Don't you eat breakfast every day?" I hear you ask.
Stay with me here.
During the pandemic, there was a time when you could meet up outside in small groups. In our local park, a genius entrepreneur parked up a coffee truck and made a small fortune furnishing people who stood in all weathers so they could get out of the house or see family. I would walk to the park every Friday and drink coffee with my parents while standing the expected distance away for safety. We stood in the wind, rain, snow, and sun. It became a mini tradition if you like.
Once the restaurants opened (for outside dining) the three of us started going for breakfast. We'd sit outside huddled up against the elements tucking into bacon and egg.
The beauty of working for myself means I'm in control of when and how I work.

I don't work on a Friday!

Instead, I meet up with my mum and dad for 'Friday Breakfast' and put the world to rights.

I used the power of storytelling to do several things:

- Engage with my audience – the comments flooded in about parents, memories of the pandemic and how others coped, working for yourself and the benefits, nutrition, and even a few people rethinking their working hours.

- Sharing basic information – I don't work on a Friday. Instead of sharing a mundane post about my opening hours, I used a story to explain why I only work four days a week. My audience will remember this story over a list of days and times.

- Know, like, and trust – family is important to me, and freedom is one of my core values. Sharing this simple story tells my audience a bit more about the name behind the brand.

Remember earlier in this chapter when I mentioned an illness thwarting my plans for world domination, well that's another story I use to help my potential clients get to know me. Everyone appreciates honesty and I often talk about the time I had to pivot my business to continue paying the bills and feeding my family. It is stories like this that resonate with your audience. They are able to connect with you in a human way which can be difficult when we spend the majority of our life online.

Find your own stories

Start making a list of some of your own stories in a notebook or on the 'notes' app on your phone. Keeping the list close allows you to tap into this pot of ideas whenever you need content for your social media platforms, blogs, talks, or interviews. Think about why you started running your business but remember to dig deeper into what you enjoyed doing as a youngster and if it can be relevant to your current work.

Here are a few examples for you:

- Were you a teenager in the 70s/80s? Who influenced or inspired you back then and has that impacted your decisions in life or work choices?

- What was your first job? What lessons did you learn?

- Have you travelled? Where have you been and what did you do? How has that shaped you as a business owner?

I often share in my talks that I lived in a converted cowshed for three months in the Catskill Mountains, New York State. It's a great conversation starter and allows me to branch off into various other topics related to my work. I love using humour in my content as I'm a silver lining kind of person who would rather laugh than worry!

The cowshed story comes from my time with Camp America when I was a sprightly 22 years of age and eager for adventure. I use this tale to inspire my audience to step outside their comfort zones (I write self-help books). I can also make people giggle as they picture me curled up on a bale of hay. The cowshed was, in fact, fully converted with bathrooms, bedrooms, a communal lounge, and a kitchen and housed all the international staff. It wasn't as bad as you imagine – well, almost not as bad!

How open and honest should you be?

It's a valid question to ask how much you should share with your audience, but there is no right or wrong answer. I'm a fairly open book (no pun intended) and feel comfortable sharing my personal stories. My audience knows I am a domestic abuse survivor, but I have never shared details of what I went through – and never will. That's where your boundaries come into play.

The stories you share don't have to be personal. You can stick to sharing business stories, case studies, or talking about the people who inspire or motivate you in your industry. Being visible is part of being a business owner, but how visible you choose to be is going to be unique to each of you.

Let's talk about kids for a moment. I'm a single mum of three and often talk about my children in my content. I rarely share pictures but if/when I do I ask their permission. My kids are also older (all in their twenties) and have built lives and careers of their own. My daughter, for instance, is a film production student at university and helps me create all my TikTok videos. It's only right I talk about her love of film and video as it's relevant to what I do for a living. The engagement I receive when sharing stories about my family is always wonderful, but I've seen influencers online who contend with horrific online abuse.

- What are you comfortable sharing with your audience?
- What do you want to keep from your audience?

Set your boundaries and stick to them. There are so many stories you can use to build relationships with your clients or customers without stepping over that line you've drawn.

Never be afraid to share the bad stuff! How much you want to share is, as always, up to you, but we all need to feel connected, supported, and less alone in this world. If you feel like your business isn't doing as well as it should and you see a piece of content from someone you admire saying the same things, how would you feel? Would it take some of that pressure off your shoulders knowing you are not alone? Could you reach out to that person and form a connection?

A word of caution, however. If you share too much of the bad stuff it will work against you and start to turn your ideal customer off your brand. They will start to scroll by your content and stop engaging. Mix your stories up as much as you can. Share the good, the great, and occasionally the ugly, but above all else be honest and authentic.

Why is storytelling so powerful?

Hopefully, you will have jotted down a few stories of your own as you've read this chapter. Keep adding to that list as you remember things or as new stories present themselves. If you're still on the fence about using storytelling in your business, then allow me to share a few benefits with you.

First of all, I want you to decide if you are a business that is simply selling a product or service, or if you are a business that your audience believes in, trusts, and wants to invest in.

Remember, we invest in human beings, we engage with stories, and our emotions are a huge factor in how and why we buy.

Think about the big brand TV adverts, especially the Christmas ones. Each brand tries to compete for our attention by sharing the most heart-warming or thought-provoking story they can find. John Lewis are a master of this.

You may not have the same marketing budget as John Lewis or Tesco, but you certainly have a pot of powerful stories.

How does storytelling work for your business?

- You get to share your values.
- You connect authentically with your ideal client.
- You evoke emotion and people will remember how you made them feel.
- You allow people to believe in you and your business as much as you do.
- You create relationships that are loyal to your brand.
- You captivate your audience, so they keep coming back.

Start telling your stories. Share little bits and pieces here and there to test the waters if you don't feel confident yet. Watch out for storytelling techniques the next time you scroll through LinkedIn or Facebook. How do they make you feel? Did you stop, read, and comment? What drew you to engage? The answers to all of these questions are more reasons why storytelling works.

Hook in your audience, entertain/inspire/motivate/or educate them, and start building those long-lasting relationships.

Happy writing!

19: Embracing AI: Your Friendly Guide for Small Business Owners

By Jacqueline Leake

Since we first outlined the content for the book, a whole new wave of technology has hit the business scene – Artificial Intelligence, or AI! Don't worry; it may sound fancy and futuristic, but it's not as complex as it seems. Let's look into how AI can be a game-changer for your business and how you can make the most of it to thrive in today's ever-changing market.

Understanding AI in a nutshell

Okay, so what exactly is AI? Think of it as the brainpower behind machines that allows them to do things that would typically require human smarts. We're talking about stuff like understanding and talking to people (natural language processing), recognising images, spotting patterns, making decisions, and much more! It's like machines with a bit of human-like magic.

How AI can boost your small business

1. Boost Your Customer Service: You know those helpful chatbots or virtual assistants you might have seen on websites? Those are AI-powered helpers! They're available 24/7 to answer common questions, guide customers, and keep them happy.

2. Make It Personal: AI can analyse customer data to understand their likes and dislikes. This helps you offer personalised product recommendations and marketing messages. It's like having a personal shopper for each customer!

3. Smoother Operations: AI can optimise how things work behind the scenes, like managing inventory, figuring out the best way to get supplies, and making the most of your resources. It's like having a super-efficient assistant.

4. Smart Data Insights: AI can dig through massive amounts of data to find hidden gems of information. This can help you make better decisions for your business, understand what's trending, and predict what customers might want next.

5. Super-charged Marketing: Ever wondered how to reach the right customers at the right time with the right message? AI can analyse customer behaviour and create targeted marketing campaigns, boosting your marketing efforts and making your business shine!

How to get started with AI

No need to feel overwhelmed! Take small steps to embrace AI in your business:

- Start small: Begin with simple AI projects that align with your business goals. For example, try using a chatbot for customer support or an AI analytics tool to know your customers better.

- Use AI-powered tools: Look for user-friendly software with built-in AI features. Some tools can help with project management, bookkeeping, and even crafting social media captions and hashtags!

- Amp up e-commerce: If you run an online store, explore AI for personalised product recommendations and smart pricing strategies. Your customers will love it!

- Automate marketing: Embrace AI-driven marketing platforms to create personalised email campaigns and targeted social media ads based on customer behaviour.

Don't be scared; address your concerns

It's natural to have some concerns about AI, like data security and privacy. Work with reputable AI providers and prioritise customer privacy. And remember, your creativity and personal touch will always shine through AI-generated content.

My AI experience

I've been using AI tools in my business, especially for marketing, and it's been a real game-changer! It saves me time, sparks my creativity, and helps me improve my content. I see AI as a helpful creative partner like an editor that enhances my work.

My upcoming chapter on outsourcing was written without the aid of AI and for this chapter I used AI technology to get the outline and structure and to make sure I covered the main points about AI. You need to make time to learn how to use AI tools, because if you don't give it the right parameters in the prompt, you are not going to get good output, so you need to spend time working out how to ask the right questions.

Keep learning and growing

AI is always evolving, so keep an eye on new trends and stay informed. Attend industry events and try out new AI solutions. It's like adding a little magic to your business!

Embrace AI as your business sidekick

Remember, AI is here to make your entrepreneurial journey more efficient, rewarding, and successful. Think of it as a fantastic sidekick that boosts the capabilities of your business and helps you grow, innovate, and build lasting relationships with your customers. Don't be afraid to explore AI's possibilities – it's an exciting journey worth taking!

20: SEO Foundations

By Andrea Rainsford

S EO! It's a dirty word to a lot of people. It's often called the dark art of tech and code.

"I hate SEO!" is something I hear all the time. But I'll let you in on a little secret, SEO is all about visibility. It's about being found by your ideal client. Good SEO means boosted visibility, which enables you to be found on the front pages of a search engine, which is ideally where you want to be, as well as in a social media search. Result!

SEO in layman's terms means being visible. So much better than 'Search Engine Optimisation', right? SEO refers to web traffic called organic search traffic, traffic that comes to your website from a web search. Organic search traffic is said to have a much higher conversion rate than any other form of web traffic, as the user is specifically searching for your product or service. They are seeking your solution to their problem.

SEO equals visibility

I do not believe in performing SEO-related activity in isolation, such as looking at your website's visibility on its own. If a website is having visibility issues it is rarely uniquely down to the SEO - it is often down to the foundations of the business, which is your core business strategy. I work a little bit differently at SEO Angel as I don't work on a website in isolation but work through a bespoke framework to ensure visibility in ALL areas of the business.

SEO is all about your ideal client finding you, engaging with you, and converting into a sale or purchase. There are many technical aspects to SEO too, but for now, let's focus on SEO = Visibility.

Question: Do you want to be found by your target audience?

If you DO want your business to be found, then SEO is something you can't ignore. It is vital to your success! SEO is seen to keep web results fair, with the current algorithms, and it is generally felt that sites appearing from a search are there because they deserve to be. Time and effort, along with a website that is aesthetically pleasing to visitors, correlates with high rankings.

Let's think about what a 'search' is, whether it is a Google search or a social media platform search. Every time you type a question into Google you are searching for something, and each search has a user intent. The user is invariably looking for a solution to a problem. You and your business could be that solution.

If you are not investing in SEO, then your search engine user is not going to find you. Without SEO, how would we find the websites, businesses, or information we seek on a daily basis? SEO makes it easy for users to find the information they require within a few seconds. If you want to know something, buy something, or learn something, you search for it!

Top SEO Tips

The current most important ranking factor for SEO is quality, authoritative content that your ideal client wants to read. They are looking for thought-provoking content that they want to engage with and share.

Here are my top SEO tips:

- Consider who you are trying to attract.
- What are their main pain points?
- How do you solve them?
- What solution do you provide?
- What keywords will they use to find you? (Unsure? Research, research, research!)
- Always write for your ideal client and not a search engine.
- Use killer headings. (Include keywords in your headings.)
- Don't stuff keywords into your content meaninglessly.
- Use your research in key structural areas: URL, title, headings, copy, ALT tags and metadata.
- Include internal links (these can include pages on your website) and quality backlinks.
- Consistently add quality content that adds value to your site via a blog.
- Once your blog is live, create a search console account and perform a URL inspection to index your blog with Google.

My top tip - add consistent quality content (blogs) to your website and social media channels.

Using keywords

When you created your website or social media channels, you may have had an idea of the key phrases/keywords you wanted to be found for - the words or phrases your ideal client will type into a search engine to find you and your services. If you didn't do this, now is the time to delve deeper into your ideal clients' search and buying behaviours.

- You want to think about your business niche, your USP, and key phrases you can rank and be found for. Trying to rank for high volume keywords takes a lot of time and effort, so think outside the box.

- Use keyword search tools like searchvolume.io, wordtracker.com, ubersuggest or other similar search tools to find average monthly search totals for certain niche keywords.

- Think about the words or phrases that are related to your business type or industry.

- Think about the words or phrases related to your ideal client's pain points that they will want a solution for.

- Think about the words or phrases that are affiliated with your business.

For example: Let's say your business is in coaching. There are a large number of coaches on the internet, so how does your ideal client find you? What type of coach are you? (Business coach, lifestyle coach, fitness coach, etc.) What area of expertise does your coaching fall into? Now you need to narrow it down some more!

When you search for Business Coach there are over one million results. How can you stand out to your idea client amongst all of those results? You niche further.

Let's say you are a business performance coach. This search term brings 310,000 results, so you have more than halved the one million results. Now let's say you only work in the engineering industry. When we search for a Business Performance Coach in Engineering it brings up 71,000 results. By being very clear on who you want to attract and where your expertise lies, it will enable your ideal client to find you more easily. Use keyword research tools to identify key terms to use in the structure of blog content, headings, titles, etc.

Maintaining visibility

Here are my top tips to maintain your visibility:

- Understand and get to know your ideal client and speak directly to them every time.

- What does your ideal client want to read about? What solution do you provide?

- Post regularly and consistently, don't post one month and not the next. Consistency is key!

- Plan all your content before you write it and research, research, research.

- What are the keywords and phrases that your ideal client will use to find you and your content in a search?

- Structure your content and blogs before you write - your introduction, body, and conclusion.

- Think about your topics and what value you are adding.

- Have you added keywords so search engines can you see you have a thorough knowledge of your topic?

- You need a killer heading that will not only encourage your reader to open your blog or newsletter, but you need to include keywords to ensure your content is found in a search.

- Call to action - what do you want your reader to do? Be clear about what action you want your audience to take: contact you, book a call, join a webinar, subscribe, etc.

- Remember quality authoritative content ranks highest!

- Once your blog is ready, do a URL inspection via your search console account. Index directly with Google!

21: Social Media Strategy Success Tips

By Colette Bratton

In today's society, social media plays a huge part in both our personal and business lives, and there are so many platforms to choose from, such as Facebook, Instagram and LinkedIn. Whilst some platforms are just social media, others offer additional benefits. For example, YouTube and Pinterest also work as search engines, whilst TikTok and YouTube are as much entertainment platforms as they are social media.

When you're looking to use social media to promote your business, it's important to understand what each social media platform offers in order to understand how each one can help you achieve your business objectives. The main thing to remember about social media is that it's social. The platforms give you the ability to create and share content for viewers to engage with and comment on. That's why it's useful to remember that it's not just about posting content on social media, but that replying and responding to comments in order to start interesting (potentially fruitful) conversations is also important. After all, that's why it's called social media - because it's your chance to get social with your ideal customers.

A great way to promote a small business

Social media is widely used by small business owners to promote their businesses for a number of reasons.

- It's efficient. For some businesses, certain social media platforms can provide a cost-effective way to reach target prospects and create awareness and engagement.

- It's low cost. One of the main reasons that social media is so popular with small business owners is that it offers a free way to promote a company. Organic marketing (i.e., using what the platform naturally offers without investing in any additional paid-for options) on social media is free to use to spread messages out to the wider community.

- It's flexible. Social media can help business owners work on a number of different business goals by varying the post content.

- It's full of prospects! Social media platforms offer some great ways to learn more about your target audience. For example, business owners can find online groups that contain their ideal prospects, then network in there. You can gain a lot of knowledge about your target audience by engaging in these groups and have the chance to comment on posts to offer advice and showcase your expertise in certain subject areas - you never know where that may lead.

Know your social media goals and objectives

It's important to think about how social media can help you grow your business. What do you want social media to help you achieve? And what's a realistic objective for your business?

Your target audience, their buying patterns, and the type of business you run may influence what's possible with social media. For some businesses, social media can be used to generate new appointments, plan discovery calls, take bookings and even make sales online. How possible each of those options is for your particular business will depend on what products/services you're selling, and how your customers and clients usually buy.

Some products and services can be bought 'off the shelf' without much deliberation. Others have a longer, more complex buying cycle where someone may need to find out about the business, have several conversations and do the whole 'know, like and trust' exercise before an order can even be considered. If you fall into this category and selling directly off social media isn't an option for your type of business, you can use the platforms to raise awareness and encourage a prospect to take that next step to find out more instead. This might involve starting a conversation on social media that then moves off the platform into an email/phone conversation before a sale can progress further.

What are your business objectives for using social media?

- Would you like to generate direct sales from your posts – and is that possible with your business model? Or does the sale of what you offer involve a longer buying cycle?
- Is it lead-generation you're after – to take a stream of interested prospects to the next step?
- Would you like more traffic, to help people find your website or landing page in order for them to take some action there?
- Are you wanting to collect email address to grow your database?
- Are you trying to raise awareness / create more engagement?
- Or something else? Once you understand what you'd like to achieve from posting about your business on social media, it's easier to think about your content plan and social media strategy.

Take time to learn

The best way to learn more about certain social media platforms is to spend time on them. By doing this, you'll be able to see how other businesses similar to yours use social media to raise awareness and attract new prospects and customers, to help you formulate your own plan of action. You may then decide to take a course, to help you learn more about social media and the nuances of the algorithms, in order to comprehend what each platform can really offer your business.

Prioritise the social platforms

With so many social media options, some business owners are unsure what social media platforms to take a presence on first. It's important to think about where your target audience hangs out online, because that's where you really need to be - on the same platforms as them! You also need to think about your type of business, in order to help you decide which social media platform(s) to focus on.

How many platforms is it best to post on?

There's no rule, as it really depends on your target audience – just try to be where your ideal customer is. Remember that you don't have to post on every social media platform, as some won't be the right fit for the target audience you're trying to reach.

Posting on too many social media platforms unnecessarily can be a huge drain on your time. However, it's worth noting that there are some economies of scale available, as some elements work well together, so you may find that whilst you're creating content for one platform, then it's fairly easy to create content for another. For example, using Meta's in-platform business tools, you can create a post on both Facebook and Instagram at the same time, making it almost as easy to post in two places as one.

You may also find that there are some platforms that you just don't like, or don't get on with for one reason or another. Just as we all have our individual favourite social media platforms that we enjoy spending time on, the opposite is true too. If your least favourite social media isn't an important platform for your business to be on, then you might just be able to forget about it. However, if the platform you're struggling with is the main place your ideal client hangs out, then it may be worthwhile investing in some training to help you understand more about what that social media platform can offer your business and how to start using it more effectively. You may find that, with a bit of extra knowledge, you might even start to enjoy using it!

If you're just starting out in business, are not very tech savvy or haven't done much with social media before, then it might help to just pick one platform to start with. Get confident on that one, and then add another, if you wish, when you're ready. It's better to be consistent and confident on one initially, than to be inconsistent and insecure on many when you're trying to get your business established on social media.

Once you've identified what social media platform(s) are your main priority, you could make a list of the others that you might like to try further down the line.

How often should content be posted on social media?

There are numerous articles on the internet that discuss recommendations about how often to post on the various social media platforms.

However, if you're a busy business owner, you need to be realistic with what's actually possible with the time you have available! Creating good quality content, sourcing images/videos and scheduling/posting can be very time consuming, so do what you can manage consistently (unless you've got any spare budget to employ some outsourced assistance to help you manage your social media and post more frequently) to start with.

Concentrate on consistency and quality. Be consistent with your posting and ensure your content is good quality so your target audience will enjoy your social media. Start off with a realistic posting goal and build up from there. Just like you'd build up fitness before a race, build up your social media muscles! The key to success is to start at a pace you can manage, build your skills, understand how the platforms work, and learn what results social media can generate for your own business on each platform. Then you'll be able to work at continually improving your results as you get better at managing the social media for your business.

When should content be posted on social media?

Again, it depends on your target audience. When are they most likely to be online? When might they have time to scroll? Have a think about your ideal customer to give you a gut feel. Then, use the analytics that are available on the platforms to get a true picture of when your target audience is online. That way, you don't have to guess, and can learn more about your prospects in the process.

What type of content should be posted on social media?

You might be starting to realise by now that the answer to many questions about marketing can be found by understanding your target audience. So, what type of content is your audience interested in? What do they want to hear from you about? Think about your ideal client when you're writing content and try to include different types of posts that they might find interesting.

There are lots of different types of social media content you can use. You can share latest news and exciting opportunities. Your content might share some 'behind the scenes' information about your business, or be inspirational, educational, entertaining, promotional or even require viewers to participate to create some engagement and interactivity.

Spending time on social media and seeing what content other businesses put out is a great way to help you think of your own ideas. Then create a content plan, so you're not trying to think of something to post each time.

You can re-purpose and recycle content to make your marketing easier. For example, you can tweak a blog to turn it into a number of individual social media posts, and vice versa, i.e., find a number of related social media posts and add a bit of additional copy to turn them into a blog!

And finally…

Just a few final points to consider.

- You'll have much more success on social media if you fully understand your ideal customer. You've seen how many of the answers to your strategic social media questions involve understanding your target audience. If you've not taken time to work on your ideal customer avatar, then it's worth making it a priority.

- Don't forget to measure your success. It's easy to spend hours on social media for little business benefit. Check if your social media is working hard enough for the hours you're investing in it. Make a note of the important social media and business statistics, to help ensure your social media results are moving you closer to achieving your business objectives.

- You may even want to consider incorporating some sponsored social media activity, such as Facebook or LinkedIn advertising in addition to your organic activity.

Whilst most of us have grown to love social media, remember there are plenty of other online and offline marketing options too. Take some time to think about your ideal customer, to help you to decide the most effective place to put your marketing messages.

22: Outsourcing

By Jacqueline Leake

The dictionary definition of outsourcing is defined as 'to contract out jobs or services to an outside supplier'. It generally means hiring an expert in a field for a task or project that you can't do, don't like to do, or frankly, shouldn't be doing.

Depending on where you are currently in your business, and your skill set, you may be considering whether or not it makes sense to start delegating or outsourcing specific tasks in your business. Or you may have already outsourced and not realised it, such as a web designer for your website. Other examples of outsourcing could be a bookkeeper, an accountant, a copywriter, or a virtual assistant, to name a few.

Every part of your business is essential, but some things are worth paying someone else to do for you, and you can create some really successful partnerships by finding the right outsourcing partner.

"47% of small business owners are too overwhelmed managing the day-to-day aspects of their businesses." Source: Microsoft small business study

Benefits of outsourcing

There are many benefits to outsourcing and delegating if done correctly, such as more time to focus on revenue-generating tasks and better use of your time. Also, supporting peak times in your business or giving yourself a break, and we all know how important that is to our mental health.

Freelancers provide flexibility allowing you to mix and match the skills that your business needs as they typically specialise in one area. They will generally charge you on a project base or an hourly rate. The truth is you cannot be creative when you're overworked, your mental health can suffer, and you want to enjoy running your business.

Outsourcing can actually save you money, yes, really, by freeing up your time to spend working on your business instead of in it. Plus, it may be a cost-effective solution rather than employing someone and all the cost that entails. You only pay for the work they do; you don't have to pay for things like taxes, PAYE, statutory holidays, annual leave, sick pay, training, or office space and equipment. You only pay the agreed amount for the work undertaken and nothing else; this can be considered a business expense, meaning you can save tax on it.

For example, if it's not your area of expertise, such as designing your website, just think how much time it would take you! Finding the right theme, designing it, and making the pages and links work could take forever and hold you back in your business, whereas paying for someone to set it up for you would be a far better use of your time and money.

The value of outsourcing

It would help if you looked at the expense of outsourcing as an investment to allow you to make more money. However, if you say, "Oh, I can't afford to outsource," and try to do it all yourself, your business will plateau as there are really only twenty-four hours in a day. Paying someone else to do the work for you can free up your time to work on generating income for your business. See the blog outsourcing example below:

Yearly Outsourcing Example

Task	Time it takes you	Time it takes outsourcer	Outsourcer hourly rate	Your hourly rate	Total Money & time saved
Monthly Blog writing	4 hours per blog 1 per month 12 per year	3 hours per blog 1 per month 12 per year	£40	£50	£960 48 hours

What it costs you in time to do the task per year: 48hrs x £50 = £2,400
What you pay to outsource the task per year: 36 hrs x £40 = £1,440
Total cash saving: £960
Hours saved = 48 (where you can earn at your hourly rate and generate more revenue equal to £2,400)

Looking at the example above, you've got forty-eight hours back as you are not doing the tasks, which is the equivalent of £2,400.

The cost to outsource the task is £1440 as it only takes the outsourcer thirty-six hours, earning you back £960 and forty-eight hours where you can earn at your hourly rate, or spend that time with family or friends, or however you like.

What should you outsource?

In essence, there are two types of outsourced tasks - the 'Work' and 'Business Development'.

The Work is the tasks that clients are already paying you to do, and Business Development is the tasks that grow your business or are necessary, e.g., marketing/accounts/sales.

Look at:

- What eats your time?
- What don't you like doing?
- What tasks you don't have the right skills for

Next decide:

- Which tasks are essential for your business and can't be done by anyone else but you
- Which tasks are essential and could be done by someone else
- Ideas and tasks that you have but don't have time to do

How to prepare your business for outsourcing

When considering what to outsource, write down ALL the tasks/projects in your business. Think about your business processes and create a manual. These are known as SOPs, Standard Operating Procedures, and are living documents that you will constantly be refining as your business evolves. To create an SOP, you can record a video showing what you do or write a step-by-step procedure, as long as you get it down so that you have a documented process of instructions to share with your outsourcer. Believe me; they will love you for it.

How to work with an outsourcer

Communicate, communicate, and communicate with your freelancer.

- Have contracts/agreements in place.
- Respond to your freelancer promptly when they have questions or seek approval for work.
- Provide and ask for feedback.
- Have your SOP instructions ready.
- You can always start with a small project until you feel more comfortable.

A freelancer is used to being their own boss and has a reputation to keep up, so usually this means they are motivated to deliver quality work on time.

How to find someone

Finding the right person to fit with you and your business:

- Look at your current networking groups. Is there the type of outsourcer you need amongst your contacts? Ask for recommendations from your peers.

- As such, a freelancer does not have to be near to you as they work remotely, but you may prefer someone close so that you can meet up.

- Get to know your freelancer and ask about their business and experience.

- Do they have the appropriate insurances?

- What tools do they use?

- Check what policies they have.

- Have a chat with them and get to know them, and always go with your instinct.

Remember, a freelancer is not a part-time employee or a temp; they are self-employed professionals who have a vested interest in the success of your business and offer a trustworthy, confidential, responsive service that will meet your business needs.

What to do when things don't work out

You may not get outsourcing right every time, and if it's not worked out for some reason, that's where having the proper contracts in place is your friend. If you *can* resolve any issues by communicating clearly, it's worth a try, but if you feel you need to part company, then do. Importantly, learn from the experience and don't give up on outsourcing. Look at what went wrong and why and make necessary changes before trying again.

I hope that I have given you a good overview of outsourcing and you won't hesitate to consider it as a sensible course of action for your business. As a Virtual Assistant myself, I can say first hand from both points of view how much outsourcing benefits both me and my clients. It is, of course, my bread and butter, but I truly see what it means to my clients when they share their workload and have a trusted person working with them in their business. As for myself, I know where my strengths are and how I want to spend my time in order to grow my business, so outsourcing just makes sense.

23: Dealing with Stress in Business

By Sharon Taylor

When you're self-employed, how you feel affects how you perform at work and how you interact with customers and clients. When you're feeling confident, in control, and have a positive, can-do attitude, this reflects outwardly, and people want to collaborate with you. Equally, when you're feeling frazzled, worried, overwhelmed, or stressed, these feelings will also spill out into your work life and affect your ability to perform and connect favourably with your current and potential clients.

What is stress

The World Health Organisation (WHO) defines stress as 'any type of change that causes physical, emotional, or psychological strain. Stress is your body's response to anything that requires attention or action.' (https://www.who.int/news-room/questions-and-answers/item/stress)

When you're stressed, your body responds by producing hormones designed to protect you when you perceive a threat to your survival that prepares you to fight, flee or freeze. It's important to remember that what causes one person to feel stressed may not have the same effect on another. From time to time, we all experience degrees of stress and something that causes a stress response today, may not have the same effect at another time.

People talk about good and bad stress. Good stress is a healthy level of stress which makes you feel energised, motivated and alive. This pressure pushes you to do something outside your comfort zone and you feel excited and positive about it. Bad stress is when your body is in a constant state of preparing to fight, flee or freeze. This is when you need to take action to recognise what your stressors are and put strategies in place that will get you on the road to feeling positive, alive and back in control again.

As a busy business owner, experiencing a degree of stress is normal as you try to navigate all the responsibilities of running your own business. Good stress will motivate you to do what's needed to move your business forward in the right direction. When you start feeling overwhelmed by the pressure of your responsibilities, your stress responses will typically manifest in some of the ways listed below.

Thoughts and feelings	Behaviours	Physical responses
• Feeling nervous, anxious, worried, or depressed. • Loss of sense of humour. • You feel uninterested in life. You're unable to enjoy yourself. • You feel overburdened. • You're easily irritated. • You find it hard to switch off. • Decision-making is hard. • Concentration is difficult.	• You find yourself avoiding situations. • You find yourself snapping at others. • You eat or consume alcohol more than usual.	• You feel tired all the time. • Your breathing is shallow. • You grind your teeth. • You're unable to get a good night's sleep. • You suffer with constipation and/or diarrhoea. • You have headaches and/or chest pains. • Your blood pressure is high.

Whether it's work- or home-related stress, feeling stressed will have a detrimental effect on your morale and level of productivity. Your ability to collaborate with your current clients, connect with potential clients and produce your best work will suffer. Once you can recognise changes in your behaviour and you can attribute them to being stressed, you can make the decision to make changes and start creating healthy habits to reduce, and more importantly, manage your stress levels.

Managing your stress effectively will help you to: –
- Build your self-belief
- Increase feelings of self-worth
- Create mental focus and clarity
- Promote a positive mindset in your work and home life

A lack of self-care

Many of my clients are busy businesswomen who are self-employed or in senior management roles. They come to me because they are feeling frazzled, overwhelmed, are experiencing re-occurring migraines or physical ailments or they are just struggling with the pressures of being a busy business owner. In addition to running a business, they usually also have responsibilities for childcare, running the household, diary management for their immediate family and sometimes wider family members too. They are spinning lots of plates and their to-do list is forever growing. They come to me for a course of reiki or reflexology treatments to help them feel mentally and physically relaxed in the hope that this will help them to get all the things on their to-do list done.

At their first session the consultation includes what they wish to get out of their course of treatments and what they are currently doing to support reaching this end result. After chatting to them it's evident to me that many of them lack a self-care routine. Regular time for themselves is nowhere on their to-do list and this is contributing to their stress levels. Looking after themselves on a regular basis is so important and something I encourage all my clients to do.

There will always be times in your life when you experience feeling overwhelmed, stressed or anxious. Having a regular self-care routine will help you feel relaxed, confident and able to cope more effectively with stressful situations when they come along. Having me-time that is consistent and suits your lifestyle is essential. As a self-employed businesswoman, looking after yourself and having me-time should be considered just as important as an appointment with a client.

What does self-care look like?

This is personal for everyone and depends on what you like doing but should be time that's just for you, away from work and gives you time away from focusing on family responsibilities. It's important to remember that self-care is not just bubble baths and candles. Although they are very nice, self-care is about nurturing your mind, body, and emotions on a regular basis. I encourage my clients to include some form of self-care as part of their daily routine.

When I start working with clients, I share how important self-care is for their mental, emotional and physical health, especially when they are a business owner and all the services they offer are provided by themself. I ask them questions to establish:

- what their current self-care routine looks like
- what self-care activities they have tried in the past and
- how these activities have worked for them.

Using the answers to these questions as a starting point, we can start creating a self-care plan that works for them and their lifestyle. We focus on what I consider to be the three primary areas of self-care – mental, emotional, and physical.

Firstly, we brainstorm to create lists of activities for each category. Then we broaden these lists by adding in anything that they like doing and use mind-mapping to extend these activities even further.

Examples of activities for each category are given below:

Physical Self-care	Mental Self-care	Emotional Self-care
• Physical exercise (running, cycling, gym, dancing, sport) • Pampering treatment (massage, holistic treatment, manicure, hot baths, hair appointment) • Eating a healthy diet • Staying hydrated • Getting enough sleep • Get regular health checks	• Meditation • Being mindful • Practice yoga or tai chi • Stroke a pet • Go for a walk in the fresh air • Put on some relaxing music • Reach out to a friend • Watch your favourite film • Do something crafty that keeps your mind focused	• Reach out to a friend • Watch an uplifting film • Listen to an inspiring podcast or TEDx talk • Declutter a space in your home • Keep a gratitude journal • Take a social media break • Read a book • Practice breathing exercises

Finding time for me-time

1. Learn how to delete and delegate – you don't have to do everything and everything doesn't need to be done. This includes activities at home and at work. Make a list of all the things that you must do and where possible delete or delegate things that don't need to be done by you. Can the children tidy their toys away? Are there any work tasks that you don't enjoy or you're not particularly good at that you can outsource?

2. Ask for help – doing this will give you time to do the things that need to be done by you and reclaim time to do things you enjoy doing. Can your children have tea at a friend's house once a week, and you reciprocate on another day? Can your partner prepare the evening meal a few times a week?

3. Set boundaries – boundaries form an important part of our self-care. As well as helping to improve relationships, boundaries help to manage the expectations of others, build self-respect, and strengthen your self-esteem.

We use all this information to map out a 28-day plan which includes all their daily activities and non-negotiable time to themselves for their self-care. The whole plan is unique to each person, and it needs to be Specific, Measurable, Achievable, Relevant and Time-Based (SMART). It's a good idea to evaluate and re-adjust the plan where necessary to make sure it's still a good fit and sustainable.

A few things that help you to stay on track include:-

An accountability buddy – someone who you can check in with about your self-care, or if you don't have someone who you can do this with, use a self-care journal.

Have routines, morning, evening, work, and downtime routines.

Be kind to yourself. At the start of your self-care journey there will be times when you're not able to do all the things you've planned. Don't be too hard on yourself. Journal about how this makes you feel then journal about how you will get back on track. More tips on journaling in chapter 25.

24: Mindset Matters

By Dr Vicky McCaig

When planning this chapter, I decided to pick the brains of the lovely ladies who are part of this business group and gain insights from the women who are out there doing it. Their length of time in business ranges from three to thirty-plus years. With such a combined wealth of knowledge, I couldn't pass up the opportunity to gather their insights.

What does mindset mean to you?

The Oxford English dictionary defines mindset as 'a set of attitudes or fixed ideas that somebody has and that are often difficult to change'. However, evidence shows you can learn to shift your mindset if you adopt an approach that fits you, and you work on it consistently. Believing you are stuck with a fixed mindset that is difficult to change is an outdated and unhelpful view. With the recognition of 'neuroplasticity' we now know that we can affect meaningful change in the neural structures of our brains by changing what we think, feel, and do. This is much more hopeful news!

"Mindset is the internal dialogue you have with yourself. The inner voice, which is responsible for keeping you on track, helping you make decisions or not. Your internal compass." – WBN
Member

Social media is filled with mindset challenges claiming to help you 'change everything in just five days.' There is nothing wrong with this if you find it supportive, however, you could risk spending a lot of time waiting until you have achieved this magical 'mindset shift' before you feel able to move forward with your business. There is no arrival point where you have your mindset all worked out. Your whole life is a journey of which your mind is a part. Some days will feel like it is working for you, and everything falls in to place; other days may feel like it is working against you, and nothing goes right.

"Many people don't understand the intrusive thoughts which come with mindset and what their purpose is. It's a psychological tool to keep you safe. The only time your brain believes it's safe is when it is working with the known. When outside your comfort zone, you feel unsafe. When people get the collywobbles, it's your brain's way of saying, 'That's scary, come back here!'" – WBN Member

There is a saying that 'we were born to survive not to thrive'. In basic survival terms, it is better to miss out on the carrot dangling ahead than lose sight of the stick beating you from behind. Anything novel or different gets put in the risky category, including the idea of stepping out and running your own business. Many of the ladies I spoke to emphasised that mindset was a crucial element in running a business. They felt it was something which needed considerable, ongoing work. If this feels like an area of struggle for you, you are in exceptionally good company.

Harness the power of values

Days when you feel you are not achieving your business goals as fast as you would like can really impact your mindset in a negative way. I want to give you a little mindset tip. Be clear about what your personal values are and how they embed within your business. Your goal might be to make a certain amount of profit, but your value might be that you want to do this with integrity whilst helping other people. Goals are something you can achieve; they have an arrival point whilst values are something you can live by in every moment of your life (your guiding light). This is important in business as there are likely to be days where you do not achieve the goal (making profit), but you can ALWAYS do things which achieve your values. Experiencing success by achieving your values every day is key to maintaining a helpful mindset to drive you forward.

To explore your values, try the following exercise:

- Imagine your great-grandchild (or someone else important in the future) is looking at old photos of you and describing you to someone else. What would you hope they would be saying about you? How would you like them to be describing your character, the type of person you were, and how you chose to live your life?

Understand the difference between beliefs and facts

"You must acknowledge that, while your voice is a powerful voice, it is not objective but completely subjective. How do you know it is true, honest, and real?" – WBN Member

If we are not careful, we can go through life simply believing everything our mind tells us without questioning its validity. This is a normal human characteristic. Before we know it, the belief has led to action, and the action becomes an unhelpful habit which is hard to break.

"I think about ingrained beliefs and things I have grown up with, things I have heard from parents and friends." - WBN Member

As you grow your business it is important to gain self-awareness by identifying how ingrained beliefs continue to play out and have an impact. Learning to identify the 'baggage I carry' as one lady put it.

"I have always seen myself as not quite good enough to do Latin and it's still there." - WBN Member

While not being chosen to learn Latin at school may not seem relevant to the business world, for this lady it led to beliefs of not being good enough, which have continued to play in her mind for many years.

As you set out on your business journey, now is the time to evaluate the challenging thoughts and beliefs that may arise by asking yourself the following questions:

- Where do I think this belief stems from?
- When did it first appear and who might have said it (whose voice is it really)?
- Is there evidence it is fact or is it fiction?

The alternative frame

Another strategy is to put a unique perspective on the unhelpful thought or belief. I call this putting it in an alternative frame. One lady I spoke to said she struggled with her confidence due to thoughts of being *'too old to change her career so late in life and start her own business'*. An alternative frame on this would be 'her life experience has made her clearer about what she does and does not want, so she is more ready to make changes'.

Try using the following prompts with unhelpful thoughts:

- Imagine it is a friend you really care about saying it to you. What would you say in return?
- Imagine you are still listening to this thought in a year's time, five years' time, ten years' time – what opportunities might you have missed? What alternative frame is more likely to lead to the action you want?

Drop the struggle

"It has taken a long time but, because of my level of self-awareness, I can step away from myself .... I can do things despite the thoughts in my head" – WBN Member

There is a saying that 'what you resist persists'. Sometimes, the more you try to ignore, quieten down, or put an alternative frame on a troubling belief or thought, the more it seems to come back harder at you. I advise trying to step back and take an observer position on the thought.

Try saying the script below to yourself and replacing the italics with your own words:

"I notice I am getting that thought again that *I am not good enough to run a business.*"

"I know that this comes from *me not being good enough to study Latin at school.*"

"Thank you mind for reminding me of this."

"I know this is not a fact and I *value tackling challenges in my life so I can really help others.*"

"I am going to choose to get on with this even while you are playing that same old story in the background."

You could also adopt a 'yes - and' approach.

"Yes, I may have this doubt in my mind AND I still choose to take action in the direction I want."

What tends to happen is that once we stop the struggle with the thought or belief, it quietens by itself.

The reversal

Sometimes, our minds can play games with us by creating subtle traps that prevent us from progressing despite trying all these strategies. In this case there may be psychological reversal happening. This is where we subconsciously perceive a downside to getting what we want. For example, someone may hold the belief that if they were successful in their career as a motivational speaker, they may have to spend more time away from their family.

Try asking yourself the following questions to identify any psychological reversals you might have:

- If you were to get what you truly desire in your business, what might you miss about how life is for you right now?
- What might you have to give up to achieve what you want?

Allow positive experiences to sink in

I am a great advocate for practicing mindfulness and trying to remain more grounded in the present moment. If we are not careful, we can spend too much of our time living in the past, or the future, where a host of anxieties can lie. Psychologist, Rick Hanson, outlines how we can rewire our brains to make the most of positive experiences, allowing them to be a buffer for the negative. Our brains tend to be Velcro for the bad and Teflon for the good, but we can actively do things to counteract this with a little bit of effort.

- Repeatedly put yourself in situations where you create the opportunity to have different experiences.
- When you experience something good, allow yourself ten-to-twenty seconds to REALLY pay attention to it, what it means for you and how it makes you feel.
- Once you have enriched the experience, take a deep breath and imagine yourself taking the experience inside and absorbing it, so it becomes part of who you are.

Choose carefully where you hang out.

"It's all about energy." – WBN Member

We are greatly influenced by our environment, including people we come across, both in person and online. With online networking there are many groups relating to women in business, and it can be hard to know where best to spend your time. It has become clear to me that some of these places can be supportive and others less so.

One WBN member talked about how it has taken time to build up what she describes as an inner circle:

"They are people I absolutely trust to be honest with me. Not just telling me what I want to hear. They tell me it as it is. We touch base on a regular basis. It is my external touch point which keeps my mindset honest and real."

Tips for choosing the right group for you

- Explore groups and get a sense of what they are like before you commit to anything. Many bona fide groups allow trial access so you can decide if they are a good fit for you.
- Reach out to other women in the group to learn more about it from their perspective and to get a sense of whether you can relate to them.

Final words from the WBN ladies

I asked, "If your younger-self were sitting in front of you now, and you could give her a piece of advice about mindset in business, what would you say?"

"Try it – you can do it! You can end up regretting so many things, and if you just did it, it would work out."

"You think there is all the time in the world but one day it could hit you – why did I stay in this job?
Believe in yourself and push yourself out of your comfort zone."

"You have an internal dialogue. Don't deny it but don't believe everything it tells you. Critically analyse what you are looking at."

"It's not what you know it's who you know. Network."

"Find out as much as you can early on. Don't make assumptions that what you have now is what you need to settle for."

"Trust your gut. Consult others but go with what makes your heart sing."

25: Journaling for Motivation and Inspiration

By Karen Hagan

Journaling is keeping a written record of your thoughts and feelings, as well as what happens in your day-to-day life. You can also include important events or occasions that you want to note. It's a way to track your life and your feelings, what makes you tick, and what makes you happy or sad.

Most people recommend journaling daily, but you can do it as and when it suits you. If this is weekly or fortnightly this is fine as there are no rules on when to do it, it is just whenever suits you best or if you feel like it.

Doing this regularly can help you understand and manage your feelings and can also help you to develop better ways of dealing with them. Often just writing them down can help you to process any feelings you don't know how to deal with.

There are lots of benefits to journaling, it can reduce stress and anxiety and has even been proven in a US study to strengthen your immune system! It also helps improve your memory. By journaling regularly, you can track any triggers which make you feel a certain way. You can also monitor your own behaviour and responses to triggers.

Other ways of using journaling

You could even use your journal as a food diary to track weight loss, or any digestive issues or potential food allergies by recording what you have eaten and any effects they may have. The act of writing these down also helps with being more mindful about what you eat. In the same way, you could record any exercise you take and note any progress or changes to your body.

Journaling for a positive mindset

Journaling helps to identify negative thoughts and behaviours and can improve your self-belief by tracking your progress and helping you to see how far you have come or how much you have improved in a certain area.

You can track improvements and changes in yourself and your life. You will find it helps you make better decisions as you will be more informed about what has led you to a certain conclusion, mindset, or choice.

This can help with mental health and depression as you can see what hurdles and problems you have managed to overcome, giving you greater self-belief and potentially making it easier to overcome future issues. You can give labels to your emotions and get them out of your head and down on paper which can be very therapeutic.

Tracking your progress

It helps you look at where you are now and where you have come from. You can note where you want to be in the future and track the journey to your goal.

You should note down your goals in your journal and refer back to them from time to time and tick them off when you have achieved them. This can help your well-being and give you a sense of pride at what you have accomplished. These goals can be short-term, medium-term, and long-term.

How to journal

Get an A5 or larger notebook. It doesn't have to be anything fancy but if you love your fancy stationery like I do, then get something that you love and that you want to pick up each day! Get a reliable decent pen, not a scratchy old biro, a pen that you enjoy using, which writes easily and fluently and doesn't shed pools of ink everywhere.

When you journal each day, start by writing down the date.

One idea, and something I do is to make the page on the left of the notebook into a monthly diary – start by putting a heading, e.g., **March**, and then write the numbers **1 to 31** down the left-hand side in a column. You can easily add events or noteworthy meetings, appointments, etc, which are happening in that month alongside each date.

On the opposite page write a 'to-do' list for that month. This could be a list of work or personal to-dos. The dates can then also be filled with a general overall feeling for each day, which you can do at the end of that day, e.g., 'emotional, sad, happy, productive', etc.
Make some other pages into 'topic' pages. For example, I have a 'menu' page. This has a list of family meals I could cook during the week and acts as a reminder if I get stuck for what meals to

cook when I feel overwhelmed or really busy. For example, spaghetti bolognese, chilli con carne, lasagne, etc., and then you can add to it with a regular favourite when the family enjoys a particular meal you have cooked.

Another page could be on the topic of **self-care ideas.** These can be useful when you feel particularly stressed, or overwhelmed, you can use this as a reminder of ways to take care of yourself. For example, you might write down 'take a day of self-care', or 'take a duvet day' or 'have a massage', 'get nails / facial done' or 'go shopping/lunch with a friend'.

A further page could be on the topic of **positive affirmations**. When you are relaxing you can repeat these to yourself, and this can give you emotional support and a positive mental attitude. An example is 'I can do anything I put my mind to', etc. You can find lots of these on the internet.

Have a topic page with a **Bucket List** of places you want to travel to. You can look back at this and tick off places as you complete them. This can help you to see what goals and dreams you have achieved already and what goals are left to realise.

You might like to write down a **Morning Routine**. This could be a range of healthy habits or things to improve your wellbeing or energy when you start the day. List the routine you would like to follow every morning before you start work. These might vary from drinking a large glass of water on waking, to exercising, meditating, reading, eating a high-protein breakfast, or listening to a podcast/audio book.

You can also buy ready-made off-the-shelf types of journals, e.g., Gratitude Journals, Mindfulness Journals. These often have inspirational quotes and pictures and can help foster a feeling of appreciation and prevention of negative thoughts.

Personally, I just use a standard notebook but generally in an elegant style or quirky designed cover. I also keep a yearly **focus sheet** in my journal at the back. I create a new one at the start of January to focus on areas for the year to come. As part of this focus sheet, I include some data collected from the year just ended. For example, in the focus sheet that I made on 1ˢᵗ January, I made four headings: Wins, Learns, Focus and Challenges.

Under the heading of wins, list as bullet points all the achievements you had during the previous year. Under learns put what you learned in the year just gone.

Focus is a list of the things going forward in the new year that you want to achieve or work on, e.g., training/qualifications, get more clients, etc.

Challenges is a list of those things you found really difficult in the year just gone or things that knocked your confidence, e.g., bad feedback, a time when a client grumbled about something, or a time when my service was not as perfect as I felt it should have been.

Each year then when you make a new focus sheet you will be able to look back and check on the sheet from previous years and see how far you have come. You will be hugely informed by the historic information in there, for example previous challenges you noted will make you realise that these 'gremlins' have been dealt with, and you have learnt from them to make your life/work/relationships so much better than before.

When you do this focus sheet, you should also include details of what support you will need to achieve these areas under your focus heading. When you look back next year you can see if you actually implemented this support and what difference it made. Or if you didn't, why not, and you will realise you perhaps should have asked for more help or delegated/outsourced more. You will also realise what you need to learn and where your weaknesses are. The feedback will be so much more tailored and personal to you because you know yourself better than anyone! And it will be received better by you because it's from you!

Be as objective as possible

Don't be too hard on yourself and don't lose sight of your best qualities – ensure you put plenty of detail under the 'Wins' section as there will be many Wins. We are notoriously bad as women for not celebrating our wins, but this is very important to do so especially in your journal to look back on and to improve your confidence and understanding of your strongest skills and talents. It can be most effective if you journal daily for about twenty minutes. But any time you can spare to do it, no matter how short will be useful.

First start by doing a brain dump, get all your thoughts and feelings down on paper.

If you struggle sometimes to sleep, put it next to your bed with a pen and when you can't drop off write down the thoughts in your head and you will then be able to sleep. Journaling is personal relaxation time. Make a cup of tea and relax and sit down to enjoy some 'you-time' which will reduce anxiety, stress, and overwhelm.

Keep it simple and don't feel like it's a chore. Add this to your morning routine before you start work or do it just before bed. There are no hard rules, just do it whenever it's best for you. You can even add doodles and drawings!

Some tips for writing in your journal:

- Things you have accomplished
- What you are grateful for

- Your desires/dreams/goals

- Your struggles

- Things you are proud of

- Inspirational quotes/motivational quotes

- What do you want your life to look like in five years' time?

Finally, remember your journal is YOURS and you can do and write whatever you want in it. Enjoy it and use it in the way it works best for you. Make it a pleasure to pick it up and read through and be reminded of your previous notes, ideas and thoughts and continue to capture in it the essence of what makes you YOU!

26: Reflect, Reframe and Reset

By Alison Taylor

All businesses need us to stand back at times and take a long, hard look at what is happening.

When and how we do that is a matter of personal choice. Too often we look backwards and make limited progress forward. We can also find ourselves on a diverging path with little chance of recovery. This may be a time when you need to connect with like-minded people, hire a business coach or have an accountability buddy to hold you to the promises you have made.

In this chapter, we are going to explore what to review, when, and how.

To hang all this together I would like you to consider the following framework devised by the lovely Kier Adair – shared here with her permission. You can connect with her on LinkedIn.

Reflect

What needs reviewing? This will clearly depend on your business service and/or product. Essentially you will want to look at:

- Initial goals – do they still serve?
- Sales
- Income
- Outgoings
- Leads gathered
- Leads converted
- Social media campaigns and numbers

- Time spent on different activities

The idea is not to beat ourselves up and definitely not compare our results with anyone else. This is our business being done by our unique-selves. Comparison is a waste of valuable energy.

The aim is to look with compassion about what is going right, what is not so hot and what needs changing. With as much of a dispassionate eye as we can. No self-flagellation needed here!

For all this to happen effectively, we need to keep good records. A simple diary, spreadsheet or notebook may suffice at the start of our journey. There are plenty of different journals that can be used to support these reflections.
Ask yourself:

- What have I learnt?
- What went well?
- Why did it go well?
- What was less successful?
- Why was it not a success?

Was it a case of being unprepared? Unsure? Did you find the task became much bigger than you expected or took you in a different direction to the one anticipated? Was there a health or family issue that derailed the plans? Did you distract yourself? Once you have the statistics in front of you, then rejoice! Smile. You have made it this far!

Do not discount or ignore your achievements. Every little success story and glimmer of optimism you have encountered will help provide fuel for the next phase. Running a business, as you have discovered, is tough. A pat on the back is no bad thing. Even if you do this for yourself.

Self-praise is okay, after all if you do not like yourself and your business offering, others will sniff out that negativity and give you a wide berth. If you can gather an accountability buddy or supportive group, then this is when they really come into their own. Choosing someone you respect and who understands your business goals and ambitions is important. Someone who is firm, reliable, and willing to challenge you.

One friend buys herself flowers each Friday if she has met her goals for that week. I would suggest if you have achieved 75% or more of your chosen weekly tasks that you spend a few moments to congratulate yourself. A hot chocolate, a bunch of flowers, a massage, a long soak in the bath or a long walk with friends. It is really important to celebrate wins. They will become your fuel and support your internal motivation.

Reframe

Looking at the successes, difficulties, and results through new eyes.

An idea has to be carried out for long enough to know if it is working or not. Expecting instantaneous results is a nonsense. Alternatively, going too long, pursing a method or idea that is clearly not working, is also energy and morale-sapping. If, however, we are reviewing regularly, both those pitfalls can be avoided.

Re-framing could involve sharing ideas with others. Exploring new options. Viewing difficulties with new eyes.

Who we surround ourselves with comes into play here. If you have read 'Think and Grow Rich' by Napoleon Hill, you will remember how he called in the help of historical successful businessmen and for each review, asked himself what advice they would have given.

The saying goes:

'we are the sum of the five people with whom we surround ourselves'.

Choosing our colleagues/business gurus/friends with care is something to consider.

Reset

This is where we consider which if any, of our statistics are not serving us or are disappointing. Does our activity now need modifying? Is the balance of our activity time right? Do we need training in an area? Do we need fresh ideas? Or perhaps we need to rethink our goals.

The brilliant business/personal development coach *Stephen Covey*, the author of *'Seven Habits of Highly Successful People',* talks about 'climbing the wrong tree'. We can be so intent beetling away at our business that it takes someone else who is watching our efforts to point out we have been climbing the wrong tree and going in totally the wrong direction.

As we mentioned, it is important to give an idea and a strategy enough time. There is a wonderful observation by an American/Finnish photographer *Arno Minkkinen* referred to in *Oliver Burkeman's* book *'Four Thousand Weeks'.*

"Originality lies on the far side of unoriginality."

Our initial idea may bear a close resemblance to other businesses. We need time to develop our own unique style. Time to allow our thoughts and creativity to mature and flourish.

Run with it!

We have to develop the power of patience. We have to go through the same steps that others may have trodden and only as we develop will our true originality evolve. We have to earn our stripes.

Merely thinking about a business idea, planning it all in our head, but never actually picking up the phone or putting the pedal to the metal can be exhausting. And gets us nowhere. We need to be active, consistently, for some time. How long that is, is down to your business plan.

We do, however, have to give a project and a strategy long enough to allow it to come to fruition. To learn from our mistakes. To find our own way of working. To evolve. If you are surrounded by supportive family and friends, that may be easier than if you are constantly having to prove yourself to the sceptics. Hence the suggestion for a business coach or an accountability team with whom you can bounce ideas.

When, what, and how?

When should all this review stuff take place?
Too much review and there will be no forward motion.
Remember you have got to pick up that phone! Consider keeping that journal, then you will be reviewing thoughts and feelings and not generalising or focusing on the most recent issues.

Looking back with clarity can be enriching

You can actually see how far you have come and how you will have grown as a person.

Other useful recording devices that you need to have to hand if the review is going to have teeth are your spreadsheets, CRM system, your diary, invoices, and bank accounts. I have always found a daybook useful. These records will help you keep track of decisions and give you the information you need to be able to fully review with honesty and not just from memory.

A daybook is an A4 book which sits on your desk with daily tasks. It allows you to record calls as they come in, ideas, formulate and make lists. These notes are then all in one place! Not on the back of an envelope, in your phone notes, or in your head! Write your to do list each evening. It will help you sleep. Write on the right-hand side of the daybook and use the left-hand side for ideas/incoming information that is useful to jot down.

How often can you review?
Weekly

- An hour at the end of each week to review goals set for the week, take a look at the accounts, money in and money out.

- A quick review of what went well. What made you smile?

- What ideas came to light as you were working?

- And finish with plans for the next week.

Monthly

- A two-hour meeting with yourself on the last day of the month will help you carry out a more in-depth review of the above points.

- Take a long hard look at the annual and quarterly goals. Are you getting closer, going round in circles, or moving further away?

- What needs introducing as you move to the next month?

- As Wendy Garcarz and Ben Hunt-Davies say, "Will it make the boat go faster?"

- Do you have some knowledge gaps?

- Do you have a skill shortage?

- What needs developing?

- Will this learning/skill development be put into next month's plans?

Quarterly

- For this review, have you thought about going somewhere different to your normal working environment?

- There are many companies offering room/workspace to hire where you can take a long hard look without being disturbed or distracted.

- The review now needs to be broader and deeper - half a day.

- Go back over the statistics.

- What new leads have you made?

- What learning has been achieved?

- What are you pleased with?

- How are the income and expenditure figures looking?

- Can costs be cut? Does financing need addressing?

- What investments need to be made in equipment, resources, time?

- And skills. Do you need to invest in some training?

- If so, what, why, and when will you do this?

- What will it help you with?

Annually

- Review everything from the quarterly review and more.

- Look at each review from the last 12 months.
- Congratulate yourself on what you have learnt.

And what happens now?

- You go on to conquer the world!
- Keep in touch. We would love to hear how it all pans out.

27: Lessons Learnt in Business

By Jules White

There's no such word as can't. I know this is true because my dad told me. If I ever told him, "I can't do this," "I can't go there," or, "I can't say that," he would tell me every time, "There's no such word as can't."

My dad features in this story because he was just the most amazing dad and was also my inspiration. From when I was a very small child, my dad ran a shop, a newsagent. I watched him serve his customers and I watched him build relationships, and for me that's where I fell in love with sales. I also fell in love with the idea of being an entrepreneur as that was exactly what my dad was.

I want to take you to 2005. Picture the scene - it's 7:30am in the morning and I'm sitting in my dining room in my dressing gown. I was there because I was running a business. My five-month-old baby was asleep upstairs - he was just three months old when I started my business. Well, that's what you do isn't it, when you've just had a baby!

I loved being a mum and I was completely in love with my son, but I knew that I was also very driven, and I would have to do something else as well as being a mum. I couldn't just be Sam's mum; I had to be working too. I started to think about what I could do. At this point in the story, I'll let you into a little secret - in my early twenties, I was an Ann Summers party planner and I loved it. I was also very good at it and, alongside a full-time job, I was also a manager of an Ann Summers team and I earned good money doing so. This got me thinking.

I totally understood the party plan business model and having researched, I couldn't find a company who were using this formula to sell baby products. It made sense to me that this was possibly the answer, I could set up a party plan business selling baby products and still be with Sam. Mums love to have coffee and ideally want to bring their babies, so why not have a party at the same time. Not only that, mums could also be consultants, planning the parties, and earning money. Now, this started to become very interesting and Truly Madly Baby was born.

I went on to Mumsnet and Netmums and I started to recruit mums to go out and do the parties. We didn't have Facebook or social media in those days. It was 2005, it was old school, and I built up a small group of ladies from as far north as Scotland and as far south as Cornwall. I knew from the start I could potentially grow a national operation.

So, back to my dining room in my dressing gown at 7:30am one May morning. I'm on my computer and up pops an advert saying, "We are looking for applicants for Dragons' Den Series 2." My husband at the time, and I, had watched the first series and it was really good. I really loved watching all those poor businesspeople squirm in front of the scary Dragons, so I applied!

The Dragons' Den deal

I didn't even think anything more of it and at 9am that morning my phone rang, and it was the BBC! They said, "We love your business, can you tell us more, and could you come down to BBC Television Centre tomorrow and pitch to the camera?"

Two weeks after that I stood on a cross in front of five very rich Dragons, pitching Truly Madly Baby. What you don't know is that I was in front of the Dragons for two and a half hours but in the programme you only see fourteen minutes. If you do ever find the clip, I was so much better than you might think!

Peter Jones and the new Dragon Theo Paphitis were bidding against each other for my business, which was both unbelievable and exciting! Ultimately I ended up shaking hands with Peter Jones for a deal of £75k for 45% of my business.

The filming all happened in May of 2005 and the first I heard from Peter's people was in September 2005. As it was, my solicitor begged me not to sign the contract because it wasn't a good deal and he told me I didn't need to do it; I trusted him and turned the investment down. You need to know that by this time the programme had still not been aired and for that reason I couldn't speak about it in any way. My episode was shown at the end of October and that evening I had two and a half thousand emails drop into my inbox and even more over the following days. They were about various things from wanting to be a consultant, to wanting to sell me their products, and several people were asking about investing and how they could get involved.

Remember, by this time, I had turned down Peter Jones, so I decided to meet up and talk to the bidders. One was someone I knew and played hockey with - she was also a finance director. Every salesperson needs a finance director. She was a mum, and I knew her - it made complete sense. She came on board for the same investment of £75k and for a slightly lower percentage share of my business.

Moving forward to 2008, Truly Madly Baby had 432 consultants across the UK, from Orkney down to Guernsey. I had enquiries from America, Australia, and Europe, from people wanting to take Truly Madly Baby out to a global audience. I was wondering if I was actually going to finally achieve my world domination!

Dark times

Unfortunately, we had become a victim of our own success and we hadn't got the right foundations in place to cope with the volume of business coming in. We needed more robust systems, more staff, and more stock. My dad was my picker and packer in my warehouse and we would often work together. Dad was an amazing stock controller, but everything was very much in his head, and whilst he was totally amazing, we had to take things to the next level.

The solution was more investment and my investor agreed to reinvestment. The amount would be uncapped, but she wanted 75% of my business. From my point of view, I had pretty much built the business alone from the beginning and I would be handing over the majority share and essentially working for her if I agreed to her terms. It was a very easy decision and my answer was no. I then set about finding someone who would buy out my business partner, but sadly ran out of time, and in May 2008 she took the business into administration and closed me down. She then bought the business back and the following day continued to run it as Truly Madly Baby, Dragons' Den Winner. This was almost three years to the day from when I had stood in the Dragons' Den.

I lost everything and was devastated. What followed was a raft of challenges that almost broke me. Firstly, I had no option but to go bankrupt. In August 2008 I found out I was pregnant, which was in some ways a light at the end of the tunnel, but the same month we found out that my dear mum had breast cancer. And then things were about to get even worse, and whilst visiting her in hospital one day I started a miscarriage and was taken straight into A&E and then admitted for three days. All hopes of having another baby felt like they were lost, and the uncertainty of mum's health was a real worry. Then in March 2009 my marriage ended. I was 40 years old, a single mum, bankrupt, with no job. My priority was my son Sam, and I so I went back out into the world and found myself a job. I had a choice; either hide in the corner and never come out or get back up and start again.

I'd been in sales most of my life, so I signed up with an agency and they soon came back with a job that looked great, but sadly the employer didn't want me. They wanted someone from a specific industry that I hadn't worked in. After persuading the agency to follow up and tell them it was at least worth interviewing me I got myself an interview – well, the agency would probably like you to think they got me the interview! The good news was I got the job!

I was back out on the road as a national sales manager, something I had done ten years ago, which meant that my ego and my pride were dented. Actually, that wasn't even important at that point. What was important was that I had a job and I was building a new chapter of my life and a new career. I smashed my first-year target and the following year was made Head of Sales. Now, I was managing a team and what was even more challenging was that as a team we were missing a £6 million target by £2 million. This was huge, we had to focus on our individual strengths and I had to motivate the team to understand what sales was really about - why our ideal clients would choose us. I made sure that we never chased the target, we just focused on building relationships with our clients and sure enough after eighteen months hard and wonderful teamwork, we hit the £6 million and even exceeded it by another £180k. It was a really amazing result and I learnt so much and had even more experience under my belt. All was well and starting to look good.

In 2012 mum was taken really poorly again and in January we were told that she had advanced liver cancer and also a rare bile duct cancer. On 24th March 2012 I lost my wonderful mum.

I didn't cry. My dad was devastated, and I had to make sure he was okay, and I also had a team who I wanted to continue to nurture. After six months of not really taking care of me, I collapsed in the shower and sobbed uncontrollably, finally grieving for my Mum.

The next three years were difficult, emotionally painful, and a continuation of my journey of loss, but I always knew that I had a choice as to how I dealt with it all and I was always positive and made the most of the situations I was in. Dad was a shadow of the man he had been and cried a lot which was very painful for me and made me so sad - it broke my heart because I couldn't help him feel better. He would go every day and sit by mum's grave and whether I thought it was good or bad for him, I had to let him do what he wanted to do.

I eventually asked him if he wanted to live with me. He was lonely and so was I and it just made sense. I adored him, spoke to him every day, and cooked Sunday dinner most weeks, so not much would change, and if he got on my nerves, I would just send him to his room! He put his bungalow up for sale and we sold it really quickly, but before we could even start to look for houses, dad became very poorly. It took some time to diagnose what was really wrong. We started with a prognosis of five years to the final decision that he had an acute leukaemia, which was not quite behaving as they could recognise, and because of that, kidney failure had started and he actually had just weeks to live.

This was my darkest time. This was the time when I felt that maybe I didn't quite have the energy or courage to get back up again. This was also one of my major breakthrough points because when my mum was ill and was dying, she wouldn't talk to me about how she was feeling, and I had so many questions I wanted to ask her. I wanted to know if she was scared but I never found out. We always talked about everything but it seems she was in denial, and knowing mum, it was to protect me and not worry me.

When my dad was in the hospice, we talked about nothing else but the end of his life. He told me he wasn't scared about dying and he also planned his funeral! Typical dad - ensuring he had 'My Way' playing at some stage. I told him I didn't know what I was going to do as I did not believe I would be okay without him. He said I would be and to remember that 'there's no such word as can't', something he had told me since I was a young girl. It has become the legacy he left me and one I use every day now. He told me I must still buy the house, have a holiday, and that I would go on to do great things. I suppose in many ways I had no choice. I still had to make sure that my purpose was Sam, but on top of that I couldn't let my dad down and he had given me my instructions - typical dad. He peacefully left me in the early hours of 2nd December 2015 and I held his hand to the end. My heart shattered, and in many ways, I will never get over losing my parents, however, it was also a new beginning on my own and time to really focus, find courage, and build a new life again.

Rising from the Ashes

I bought my house, I had an amazing holiday in St. Lucia where I thought about what my next adventure would be, and in April 2017, I started my own sales consultancy. A business I would never have been able to start without the extra years of sales experience I had when I was rebuilding my career after losing my Truly Madly Baby business. Who knew that this would have been so important, and here I was able to confidently coach in the field of sales; a subject I was actually very passionate about.

What did I truly learn – well, I know that we should never live in the past. We are built from every mistake we make. Only ever look back to see how far you have come. We should also never live in the future - have aspirations and goals, but don't live there because none of us know what is going to happen next, as my story shows, and I'm sure your stories do too. All we end up doing is 'future catastrophising' and why worry about something you have no knowledge about?

What we can be sure of is the now. What we truly know is what is happening right now. You are reading this and hopefully are inspired to see that there is no such word as can't. You can have dreams, and they can come true. For me, I have created a new business and a whole new methodology around sales called 'Live it Love it Sell it'. Sales is the art of human conversation and we can all sell. This inspired me to write a book of my own, funnily enough called 'Live it Love it Sell It!'. I am also host of my very own podcast 'The Human Conversation' and just eighteen months after starting my business, I stood on stage at the largest TEDx event in Europe in Brighton, watched by 1600 people. I had become a TEDx Speaker! This was a dream and it has now come true.

You can do anything if you truly want to, and if you do one thing after reading my story, I want you to think of your dream. The one thing that you really want to do, that you may not be quite brave enough to do and I want you to ask yourself this question, "Will it be one day, or is this day one?'

You decide.

Part 3

Women's Business Network

28: Women's Business Network
Sharon Louca

Hello, I'm Sharon Louca, the award-winning founder of Women's Business Network Limited. I provide female business owners with the support they need to take back control and grow a profitable and successful business.

I started my first networking group back in 2014 as I wanted to pay it forward for all the help and support I received when starting my business five years earlier. I was new to entrepreneurship so lacked some of the knowledge and skills required to run a successful business. Through the connections, mentors and training I received from the business networking community I have gone on to run three businesses and a business centre in Staffordshire.

I continued to run monthly face-to-face groups until early 2020. When the Covid pandemic put the UK into lockdown in March 2020, I ran weekly online meetings to support my members. The pandemic created an opportunity for me to take my local networking group and introduce it to a much wider audience. We reached a global audience within a matter of weeks. As the world changed and working online and remotely became normal, I decided to launch Women's Business Network Ltd to the world.

My focus has always been on supporting women running their own businesses after experiencing first-hand the struggles and problems women face. Juggling a business alongside a home, family, and ageing relatives all present challenges and having the support of like-minded women who know what you are experiencing is so important.

Women also face financial challenges and can feel pressured to give up their business and get a job! Being torn in so many directions contribute to these feelings.

At WBN, we are far more than just a business networking group. We provide a safe space for women to focus on building confidence and self-belief, increasing business knowledge and developing strong, trusted relationships. Having a support network that gives you a true sense of belonging is immensely powerful. It can really make a difference and prevent women having to give up their dream of running a business.

Starting out, it is impossible to know all there is to know about business which is why I have a panel of experts. I invite high calibre speakers along to our monthly meetings to share their expertise with the group. We run Bootcamp sessions where our members deliver talks on their area of knowledge and experience to the other members. Knowledge is power and there is always something new to learn.

WBN supports women at all stages of their business journey and the group is made up of women from a huge variety of business sectors. We meet online via Zoom twice per month and host business clinics, member story slots to showcase our members, plus our monthly guest speakers delivering on a business or personal development topic.

We have created a fantastic community of like-minded women. I don't believe in having a one-seat policy and strongly believe in collaboration over competition. Our Bootcamp and this book are two of our collaboration projects to date with more planned for the future. We promote our members to help them increase their visibility and brand awareness through speaking opportunities, a business profile on our website, and exposure via our social media channels.

Even though the world has returned to face-to-face contact networking, WBN will remain an online support network, understanding the need to connect women nationally and internationally without the need for a physical venue.

My ethos at Women's Business Network is that no woman in business should feel alone, which is my driving force behind helping female business owners to be the best version of themselves. I want them to feel in control of running their own business, safe in the knowledge that they have the support network in place to deal with whatever life may throw at them!

Women's Business Network continues to grow and attract a global audience of women running their own businesses.

Here is a testimonial from our member *Julie Heginbottom*:

"I can really recommend any women business owners to join WBN. Sharon is so knowledgeable about business development and takes the time to get to know you and your business. I felt welcomed into the group right from the start. Members all show an interest in my work and provide encouragement and ideas on how I can move forward. There is such a range of expertise within the group that you can draw on as well as having a safe space to share. You also have the chance to experience the group a couple of times before joining, without any pressure at all."

Appendix A: Contributing Authors

Alison Taylor
[Chapters 1, 26]

'Age is no barrier'.
It is never too late to start a business.

Alison began her Forever Living network marketing career whilst still in full-time teaching. *'If you want something doing, give it to a busy person'.*
The reason for this initial dabble into entrepreneurship was to financially support her daughter's university years. Serendipity took a hand and introduced her to a health company, the perfect vehicle for her passionate love of nutrition and health.

Since 2006, Alison has loved the professional way her business has encouraged lifelong learning and introduced her to a world of supportive female business colleagues. Now a fully qualified health coach, alongside her retail and leadership roles, she has grown intellectually and emotionally, delighting in the global connections she has made.
Alison finds herself in her eighth decade living a balanced, fulfilled, and joyful life. One that is still full of possibilities.

Alison Taylor, Forever Living -https://alisontaylor.myforever.biz/taylor/

Andrea Rainsford
[Chapters 20]

Andrea Rainsford is an award-winning SEO consultant with over 25 years of business development and SEO experience, working in her corporate career with many large corporates, including Ernst & Young, and Eversheds.

Her passion is helping small businesses to thrive through visibility, to remove the tech and jargon from SEO, and make it accessible to all. Bringing her unique skills and breadth of knowledge to all her projects.

Andrea Rainsford, SEO Angel - https://www.seoangel.co.uk/

Colette Bratton
[Chapter 15, 17, 21]

Marketing trainer and mentor, Colette Bratton uses her thirty-plus years of marketing experience to help ambitious entrepreneurs use marketing more effectively to attract more dream clients and grow their businesses. She's on a mission to make marketing more manageable for small business owners and solo entrepreneurs. Colette understands how difficult marketing can be for small business owners and offers a number of ways to help make marketing easier.

Founder of the 'Marketing Momentum Training Academy' and author of the 'Entrepreneurs Marketing, Social Media & Business Planner', Colette has run her own successful marketing consultancy business since 2004. As well as marketing coaching and consultancy, Colette offers online and in-person marketing training, teaching small business owners how to use marketing effectively, including how to use platforms such as LinkedIn, Facebook, TikTok, Instagram, Pinterest, Twitter, Canva, Mailchimp, and many other tools to help raise brand awareness and generate enquiries.

Colette loves finding out about other businesses and providing ideas and inspiration to help them move to the next level. She enjoys growing her business whilst helping other business owners grow theirs.

Colette Bratton, Small Business Equaliser - https://www.smallbusinessequaliser.com/
Or connect with her on LinkedIn at https://www.linkedin.com/in/colettebratton

Ellen Badat
[Chapter 10]

Ellen was born in Gloucester and has lived there all her life. She became a company director at the age of thirty after working in various businesses in her late teens and twenties. Her previous job roles included customer services, both face to face and on the phone, marketing, accounts, sales, and back-office admin work. All these roles help prepare her for running her own business, alongside having a husband and two cats. Purple Tree Solutions provide IT support and services to individuals, sole traders, and small businesses across the UK.

Ellen enjoys helping people, solving people's tech problems and providing solutions so that they get the most from their tech and really make it work for them. The name Purple Tree Solutions, comes from, well, the fact that Ellen likes purple, and the tree represents the different 'branches' of IT that they do, tech support, email, web design, online backup, security, etc. Basically, they find the solution that works for you and your business.

Their IT support service is on a pay-as-you-go basis – no contract or retainer - so whether you are having problems with your email, printer, or just your technology in general, they can help.

Ellen Badat, Purple Tree Solutions - https://www.purpletree.solutions/ or email ellen@purpletree.solutions

Helen Chidgey
[Chapter 8]

Helen Chidgey is a Senior Leader with Tropic Skincare and has been working with the brand since 2013.

Finding solutions for people's skincare woes is Helen's passion! With an award-winning range of products to explore, she loves to guide people to a healthier, more joyful way to care for themselves that truly brings out their confidence and helps them stand powerfully as the person they are. They are also reassured that their choices are making a positive impact on not just themselves, but the planet too. Helen prides herself on offering excellent customer service and developing relationships with her customers that ensure that as life changes, their skincare and makeup routine can adapt to meet their new needs. She offers complementary sessions 1-2-1 in people's homes or online, as well as fun get-togethers which are a great way to connect with friends. Tropic fans often go on to become their own Ambassadors, and supporting them on their journey and seeing them grow and flourish is a real joy for Helen too!

Helen Chidgey, Leader Tropic Skincare - helen.chidgey@btinternet.com

https://tropicskincare.com/pages/helenchidgey

Jacky Wood
(Proof-reader)

Jacky Wood is a Licensed Menopause Champion with MEG (Menopause Experts Group Ltd), and she specialises in helping women overcome the challenges that come from experiencing negative menopause symptoms. A traumatic and protracted menopause experience inspired her to learn how she could improve her own health and wellbeing, not only at the time, but also into the future.

Menopause can affect us mentally and physically, but it doesn't have to be a distressing time of life, and Jacky's knowledge allows her to guide women to regain balance and resilience, to take control once again.

During her sessions, she first looks at the symptoms that are the most debilitating. Once uncovered, she can gradually offer plain and simple information to indicate what's causing them, then together decide what can be done to ease them, which eventually results in feelings of improved general wellbeing and optimism.

It's Jacky's view that the more we know, the more freedom it gives us to make informed choices in our best interests. Because our menopause is unique to us, Jacky's main aim is to equip people with the right information for them, and that knowledge, with self-care, will ensure a healthier existence now and going forwards.

http://helpwithmenopause.net/

Jacqueline Leake
[Chapter 19, 22]

Jacqueline Leake is the proud business owner of J Leake VA Services, which she established in 2017. As an accomplished virtual assistant, Jacqueline has been honoured with the prestigious 'Ladies First Digital Star' award in recognition of her outstanding contributions.

With a genuine passion for helping solopreneurs achieve growth and work more efficiently, Jacqueline collaborates closely with her clients. Her expertise lies in providing invaluable behind-the-scenes support that enables businesses to thrive. She excels at setting up efficient funnels, developing streamlined processes and procedures, and implementing time-saving automations. By leveraging her skills, she empowers entrepreneurs to focus on strategic aspects of their businesses, granting them the precious gift of time.

Jacqueline's areas of specialty encompass a wide range of valuable services. She is highly skilled in email marketing, ensuring impactful communication with target audiences. Additionally, Jacqueline possesses an astute understanding of launching courses, masterclasses, and digital products, creating successful campaigns. Her proficiency in developing robust systems and processes ensures optimal workflow management, enabling businesses to operate seamlessly.

Approachable and authentic, Jacqueline Leake is committed to building meaningful connections with her clients. With her friendly demeanour and unwavering support, she offers a transformative partnership that cultivates business growth and success.

Jacqueline Leake, J Leake VA Services - https://www.jleake-va-services.com/

Jules White
[Chapter 27]

Jules White is an award-winning international sales consultant with over thirty years of business and sales experience. Working in many different sectors selling everything from baby products to stainless steel to Yellow Pages she has also experienced every job role within sales, from telesales through to sales director and has a wonderful breadth of knowledge and experience to bring to her work. She also secured investment from Peter Jones in the BBC's Dragons' Den, which is the ultimate pitch to win!

Her passion and mission are to bring a new outlook and perception to sales in the modern business age we live in, which will help you to truly be unique. Jules' ultimate aim is to make sure you create an unparalleled sales experience for all of your customers through you and your unique people.

Jules is the author of Amazon Best Seller *Live It Love It Sell It*.

Jules White, Live It Love It Sell It - https://liveitloveitsellit.co.uk/

Karen Hagan
[Chapters 3, 25]

Karen Hagan (DipPFS, BA Hons), is a financial adviser and pension transfer specialist with over twenty-four years' experience in financial services, and starting out as an administrator, Karen became qualified as an adviser in 2016. Karen always aims to provide a first-class service to her clients, helping them with their financial planning, and specifically with advice on pensions, investments protection, corporate protection and long-term care fees planning. She also has a specialist qualification in looking after vulnerable clients.

Karen aims to always provide a caring and empathetic service, listening to and understanding what her clients need and helping them to achieve their objectives. It is important to her to make the whole process easy and understandable without using over-complicated financial jargon.

Outside of work, Karen has a busy family life with three grown-up children and a step-son, a cat and a dog! She also enjoys reading, knitting, and travelling, especially to European cities.

Karen Hagan, Four Oaks Financial Services - http://www.fouroaksfs.com/

Kim Masters
[Chapter 4]

Kim is the Founder of MATS Consulting and Make Peace With Money. It's safe to say that she looks at money in a slightly different way to most people. She combines her twenty-five years of accounting experience with her passion for complementary therapies, to help individuals and business-owners to improve their relationship with money.

As well as studying bookkeeping and accounting in South Africa, Kim is also qualified in Shiatsu, Reiki, and Swedish massage, and has a BA in Business Psychology.

Kim uses her lived experience to help others. In 2010, she collapsed while getting off a flight from Johannesburg and was diagnosed with two blood clots in her lungs, taking her over a year to fully recover from, which impacted her finances. Kim and her husband, Paul, were getting back on track when in 2016, Paul had a mental breakdown at work, which affected his ability to earn money.

These experiences mean that Kim knows what it is to struggle financially, which makes her able to relate to others who are in a similar position. She approaches her work in a practical, empathetic, non-judgemental way. Her mantra is to 'work smarter, not harder'.

Kim Masters, MATS Consulting - http://www.makepeacewithmoney.co.uk/

Lorraine Willis
[Chapter 13]

Credit Control is a critical part of a well-managed business and sustains and improves cash flow. After working in the financial sector for a number of years and being on both sides of the credit control process, Lorraine Willis realised there was a need for respect, patience, and tenacity in this role. More and more businesses are realising too that credit control is a time-consuming skill and is about building solid relationships with finance teams or individuals.

Lorraine prides herself on forging strong professional relationships with her customers, where she aims to resolve issues that may have caused payment delays previously, or potentially in the future. However, in the unfortunate event of non-payment, Lorraine also works alongside a no-win, no-fee debt agency that will take the matter further if needed. Throughout this process, she will collate and monitor and report where necessary so a fully bespoke package can be arranged.

Credit Control in a nutshell, 'Turnover is Vanity, Profit is Sanity, but Cash is King'.

Lorraine Willis, Simply Sutton Credit Control - https://www.simplysuttoncreditcontrol.co.uk/

Nicky Tonks
[Chapter 12]

Nicky is an extremely proud mom of two wonderful sons who are following their dreams in the big wide world, has a very supportive, caring, husband who has a passion for helping people become the very best they can be.

Nicky enjoys watching rugby, in fact most sports, and walking, Pilates, yoga, films, theatre, live music, gardening, travel, and personal development.

Nicky gets a lot of satisfaction in helping people and Utility Warehouse has given her the opportunity not only to help others but also become part of a supportive network of people who also have a passion to help people develop and grow. UW has given Nicky a way to earn an extra income by working part time alongside other commitments and receives residual income each month for work done just once.

As company secretary for Orange and Blue UK, Nicky handles the day-to-day admin and accounts, and she is also administrator for Prevue Online profile assessments.

"Whatever you vividly imagine, ardently desire, sincerely believe, and enthusiastically act upon must inevitably come to pass!" Paul J. Meyer - Founder LMI Inc.

Nicky Tonks, Utility Warehouse Authorised Partner - https://uw.partners/004590

Nina Molyneux
[Chapter 9]

Nina is a complementary therapist, teacher and mentor, who has run her own business for more than twenty years. Having started her working life in a corporate manufacturing environment, she is very aware of the pros and cons of being a salaried employee, as well as those of steering her own ship. With this, she has discovered that she is more than happy to give up the apparent security of a salary in favour of the risks and freedoms of running her own show.

She has a particular interest in developing a sense of direction, personal choice, and confidence in her clients via the medium of embodied presence and awareness. She applies this approach to her therapeutic work and more recently through training and consultancy for business owners who are keen to foster an authentic leadership style which effortlessly reflects their values and personality.

Nina believes wholeheartedly that business should work for us rather than vice versa and has shaped her own working life to suit the shifting influences of family responsibilities and personal needs as they have changed over time.

Nina Molyneux, Embodied Business Limited - https://www.embodiedbusiness.ltd/

Sarah Gray
[Chapter 7]

Female business owners don't have to be afraid of increasing their visibility on or offline. Sarah Gray, Style Confidence Coach, works to help them to become style confident offering the most effective personal style tools and services to help them get there.

Sarah's natural intuition and vast experience enables her to put every client at ease, to allow them to look at themselves in a positive way and to develop a personal style unique to them. One that reflects their personal and business values so they can confidently increase their visibility and fearlessly show up as the expert they are.

Sarah says,

"Comfort zones are pushed a little but I absolutely am not here to make you into somebody you are not. My job is to ensure you shine on the outside."

Don't underestimate the impact of impeccable styling on your business success. With Sarah by your side, you'll benefit from her extensive industry experience, knowledge of diverse body types, and style personalities. Investing in a professional stylist is an investment in the overall quality and impact of your visuals. Sarah is dedicated to helping you achieve your creative goals and surpassing your expectations.

Sarah Gray, Sarah Gray Styling - https://www.sarahgraystyling.com/

Sharon Louca, founder of Womens Business Network
[Chapters 14, 16, 28]

Sharon Louca is the Founder and Host of Women's Business Network. Sharon is passionate about helping and supporting women as they navigate their business journey. Sharon started her own business in 2009 during a recession with no clients or contacts, just a passion to help others, and a need to contribute to the family finances whilst looking after her two young boys. Sharon received so much help and advice in her early days from people who became mentors and friends.

In 2014, she decided to 'pay it forward' and started running her own networking groups from her business centre in Tamworth for local businesswomen. In March 2020, when the Covid pandemic hit, Sharon started supporting women online via free weekly meetings, and in July 2020, Women's Business Networking Limited was launched.

Sharon is now a multi-award winning business owner and uses her fourteen years of business support and quality management experience and knowledge to support women through networking, mentoring, and accountability.

Sharon is married to Spencer and has two sons Jack and Cameron. Jack has followed his parents into self-employment as a barber. Cameron is a barber and part-time DJ. Sharon loves to travel and now spends as much time as possible in Cyprus. The beauty of online working is being able to work anywhere in the world thanks to the power of the internet.

Womens Business Network - https://womensbusinessnetwork.co.uk/

Sharon Taylor
[Chapter 23]

Sharon Taylor is a complementary therapist, and she helps women to improve their mental, emotional, and physical health and wellbeing.

With more than twenty-seven therapy modalities under her belt, for the past seventeen years, Sharon has used her life skills, therapy skills, and most importantly, her listening-ear to hear women's worries and concerns. Sharon then gently guides them to increase their self-awareness and self-worth by making simple but effective lifestyle and behaviour changes.

Whether it's online or hands-on, when you work with Sharon your bespoke sessions will be designed to help you get closer to the root of what's causing you to feel overwhelmed or frazzled (because most of the time it's not because you're just feeling tired). Sharon will give you tips, tools and techniques that you can use outside your sessions that will support you long-term.

You live a busy life and you've earned the right to have some well-deserved time out for your personal growth and development.

So, if you could do with having a few more tools in your toolbox to draw on when life gets a bit fraught, get in touch with Sharon for a chat to find out how working with her can help you.

Sharon Taylor, Complete Harmony - https://www.complete-harmony.co.uk/

Shelley Wilson
[Chapter 18]

Shelley Wilson is a multi-genre author, blogger, and writing mentor. She offers guidance, experience, and accountability to her writing clients through mentoring, courses, workshops, and free resources. As an author of nineteen books, her writing clients get to see the tried and tested methods she uses to maintain a successful writing business. The mix of processes, motivational formulas, and accountability strategies Shelley shares helps her clients write their books and blogs to raise their visibility.

Shelley Wilson, Shelley Wilson Writing Mentor - https://shelleywilsonwritingmentor.com/

Shelley Wilson Author - https://linktr.ee/ShelleyWilson72

Sue Green
[Chapter 13]

Sue Green of RixGreen is an accounting software and IT trainer specialising in working with business owners and accounts teams to streamline their accounting systems using the cloud-based software Xero.

Sue is not a numbers person, which surprises her clients, because working with Xero doesn't require a head for numbers, but it does manifest a passion for business. Sue offers bespoke expert training on Xero both online remotely and onsite where she demonstrates the versatility of Xero and how it makes a difference to the business.

As a business owner herself, Sue understands the importance of having financial information available at your fingertips. Sue is a huge advocate for working smarter not harder, and her knowledge of the wide library of apps that integrate with Xero to simplify processes within the business at the click of a button makes it a real game changer.

Sue Green, Rix Green Limited - https://www.rixgreen.co.uk/

Vicky Farmer
[Chapters 5, 11]

Vicky started her working life in chartered accountancy, a role she enjoyed for thirty years, and which also included five years as a university lecturer. But in 2009, Vicky's career took a completely different direction following redundancy, resulting in her using the skills she had learned to create her own business and ultimately retraining as a nutritionist and health coach. As a result of her passion to help people optimise their health through what they eat, what they put on their skin, and how to reduce the impact of unnecessary chemicals around the home, she gives you a truly holistic approach to a healthier lifestyle, that not only works, but is also sustainable for the health of ourselves and our planet.

Vicky also enjoys baking, and is a nationally qualified judge with the Women's Institute, judging preserves and cookery at county fairs and produce shows around the Midlands. In addition, she is a big animal lover and since 2004 has been a volunteer fundraiser for Brooke, an equine charity that helps improve working conditions for horses and donkeys, and the families who rely on them, in harsh environments in some of the poorest parts of the world where they are still relied on as transport. She is also a keen quizzer and has appeared on over 20 TV quiz shows.

Vicky Farmer, Feel Good Factor - https://www.vickyfarmer.com/

Dr Vicky McCaig
[Chapter 24]

Dr Vicky McCaig is a clinical psychologist who has been working in the helping professions for over twenty-five years. She started her career in forensic settings and drug and alcohol services. After becoming a mother, she moved on to specialise in working with children and families with a particular interest in supporting those with neurodevelopmental conditions.

She worked as a supervisor and national consultant for multisystemic therapy teams in the UK for ten years before moving on to her current role. She now splits her time working as a programme manager for a functional family therapy team and seeing private clients through her online practice. She more recently qualified as a meditation teacher and KonMari consultant, and holds an interest in all strategies and techniques which enhance human energy, including EFT (Emotional Freedom Techniques) and Feng Shui.

Dr Vicky McCaig, Spark Joy UK - http://www.sparkjoyuk.com/

Wendy Garcarz
[Chapters 2, 6]

My name is Wendy Garcarz, and I lead a double life…

By day Wendy Garcarz is an author of business books, a business strategist and futurist, who uses her experience of thirty years to support business leaders to build more profitable businesses. Her latest book *Come Out Fighting* was written to help businesses recover from the pandemic, getting back into profit the quickest and easiest way.

Wendy is the founder of the Micro Business Growth Club, an online members community offering gold standard business development at a price that small businesses can afford.

By night she is Wendy Charlton who writes espionage novels that challenge the stereotypes associated with ageing and dementia. *Keeping Secrets* and *Hidden Secrets* are set in Shady Fields, a residential home for ex MI5 and MI6 agents. Now there is no cold war, our agents grow old enough to retire and draw their pension, but some of them experience memory problems. What do you do when they start to talk and share state secrets…?

Wendy Garcarz Consulting
www.wendygarcarz.com
wendy@wendygarcarz.com

The Micro Business Growth Club
www.microbusinessgrowthclub.com

Wendy Charlton Novelist
www.wendycharlton.co.uk
wendy@wendycharlton.co.uk

Printed in Great Britain
by Amazon

29281609R00097